GREAT INFIELDERS OF THE MAJOR LEAGUES

Exciting profiles of twelve stars of recent years. They are first basemen Boog Powell, Willie McCovey and Gil Hodges; second basemen Glenn Beckert, Ken Hubbs and Jackie Robinson; shortstops Luis Aparicio, Pee Wee Reese and Phil Rizzuto; and third basemen Brooks Robinson and Ken and Clete Boyer.

GREAT INFIELDERS OF THE MAJOR LEAGUES

BY DAVE KLEIN

Illustrated with photographs

RANDOM HOUSE · NEW YORK

Library of Congress Cataloging in Publication Data
Klein, Dave.
Great infielders of the major leagues.
(Major league library)
SUMMARY: Profiles of twelve outstanding major league infield-
ers since World War II.
1. Baseball—Biography—Juvenile literature. [1. Baseball—Biog-
raphy] I. Title.
GV865.A1K56   796.357'0922   70-37410

ISBN 0-394-82383-4 ISBN 0-394-92383-9 (lib. bdg.)

For Aaron,
who is always wondering

CONTENTS

INTRODUCTION

Infielders are the heart of a baseball team. They make the double plays that can end a rally and guard the basepaths to keep hits from being turned into runs. They are the first line of defense for the pitcher. Any successful pitcher owes part of his success to the infielders that play behind him.

This book tells the stories of twelve outstanding infielders who have starred in the major leagues since 1945. We have presented recent stars, including Glenn Beckert, Brooks Robinson and Boog Powell, and great infielders of earlier years—Gil Hodges,

Jackie Robinson, Ken Hubbs, Ken and Clete Boyer and others.

Casey Stengel, who achieved greatness as a player and later as the manager of the New York Yankees and New York Mets, always said the success of his teams depended on the quality of his infielders.

"You can teach someone to play the outfield," he said, "and you can teach someone to throw a curve ball, but infielders must be natural athletes. To do the things they must do requires special gifts, and no one can teach that."

There have been many other great infielders, both past and present. Some, such as Honus Wagner, Rogers Hornsby and Lou Gehrig, finished their playing careers before 1945. Many others are in the midst of great careers. But the twelve chosen represent the very best of their time, men who combined natural ability with effort and enthusiasm to gain a lasting place in the story of baseball.

GREAT INFIELDERS OF THE MAJOR LEAGUES

GIL HODGES

To baseball fans everywhere, 1969 was the year of the Miracle Mets. The miracle was easy to describe: this New York team had failed to finish higher than ninth place in any previous season. Then in 1969 it went all the way to the top, winning the National League pennant and the World Series.

To one man, the excitement of that spectacular pennant chase was not new. His name was Gil Hodges, and he was the manager of the Mets. In fact, for Hodges the year of the Mets recalled similar experiences when he was an All-Star first baseman and home-run slugger for the Brooklyn Dodgers.

Gil Hodges hugs his wife and his daughter after the Mets won the World Series in 1969.

Winning a pennant for the Mets was like coming home for Hodges. The Mets had been formed by the major leagues to take the place of the Dodgers in New York City. In 1957 both the Dodgers and the New York Giants had moved out of the city to Los Angeles and San Francisco. New York was without a National League team until the Mets came along. Now in 1969 New Yorkers not only had a team, they had a World Champion, managed by one of their old Brooklyn heroes, Gil Hodges.

Gil was a muscular 6-foot-2, 200-pounder who played 18 major league seasons before becoming a manager. He was the National League's All-Star first baseman eleven times, and he played on seven pennant-winning Dodger teams in Brooklyn and Los Angeles.

In New York and especially in Brooklyn, the city's largest borough, Hodges was a hero to millions of loyal fans. He hit 370 home runs in his career. Fourteen were grand-slam homers, still a National League record. For seven consecutive seasons Gil drove in more than 100 runs, reaching a high of 130. He played in 2,071 games in the majors and finished with a lifetime batting average of .273.

One of Gil's performances especially stands out. It was August 31, 1950, and Brooklyn was playing the Boston Braves. In this game Gil became one of only eight men in major league history to hit four home runs in nine innings.

"The odd thing about that game," Gil said later, "is that the home runs came off four different pitchers and that two of them were right-handers and two lefties. I remember after I had hit the third one, our pitcher for that day, Rex Barney, said to me, 'You haven't hit one good yet.'

"Then, when I singled in the seventh inning, I never thought I'd get a chance to bat again. But the team came up with a big rally in the eighth and I got another chance. Johnny Antonelli was pitching by then, and I really hit a good one. When I got back to the dugout, Barney smiled and said, 'Congratulations, now you really hit one.'

"It was wonderful to hit four in one game," Hodges continued, "but we won the game easily, so the third and fourth homers didn't really mean anything. The ones you remember more are the ones that do something to help the club."

Hodges was almost as famous as a fielder as he was as a hitter. Three times he led the league's first basemen in fielding average, and after his rookie season, his average never dropped below .990. A first baseman handles more fielding chances than any other player, and Hodges handled 99 out of 100 without an error.

Gilbert Raymond Hodges was born April 4, 1924, in Princeton, Indiana. "I remember playing baseball from the time I was old enough to do it," he said later. "I was always a big boy, so I had a good time hitting the ball. But I was a little clumsy, and maybe that's what helped me develop my fielding."

Hodges was born to a coal-mining family. Gil recalled, "My dad never had much time for athletics because he always worked so hard. But he encouraged me to play all the games and he was proud when I had a good day. Sports was important to him."

Gil's major league career began late in 1943 when he played in one game for the Dodgers. He was only 19 years old. But World War II was in progress and Hodges enlisted in the Marines. He participated in the invasion of Okinawa and saw other action in the South Pacific. He did not return to baseball until the 1947 season.

Hodges was a rookie all over again in 1947. He was used as a part-time catcher that year playing behind first-stringer Bruce Edwards. In 1948, however, the Dodgers signed catcher Roy Campanella, one of the first Negro players to join the major leagues. Campanella, who had been playing in the Negro Leagues, became one of the finest catchers in the history of the game, and when he came up to the Dodgers he ended Hodges' catching career.

What the Dodgers needed was a first baseman, and Gil Hodges was their man. In 1947 Jackie Robinson had played first, but at the start of the 1948 season he moved over to second base and Hodges took over first.

Campanella, Robinson and Hodges were only the beginning of that outstanding Dodger team. Other stars included Pee Wee Reese, on his way to becoming one of the game's great shortstops, and outfielders Duke Snider and Carl Furillo.

"Playing with guys like that almost guaranteed me the chance to hit with men on base," Hodges remarked later. "There was no one the pitchers could consider an

Hodges stretches for a throw from second baseman Jackie Robinson during a 1949 game against Pittsburgh.

'easy out' and so they had to pitch to me. In fact, I think they were happier when I came up than when they had to face Campy or Jackie or Duke. I was lucky to be on such teams. It made hitting easier since they couldn't take the chance of walking me and letting one of the others get me home. We terrified a lot of very good pitchers."

The Dodgers finished third in 1948, but bounced back in 1949 to unseat the defending champion Boston Braves. Gil contributed a .285 batting average with 23 homers and 115 runs batted in. He also hit a home run against the Yankees in the World Series, although the Dodgers lost in five games.

Hodges followed with another outstanding year in 1950. He hit 35 home runs, drove in 113 runs and batted .283. He also hit his four home runs in one game against Boston. The Dodgers battled to the very last day of the season, but lost out to the Philadelphia Phillies. Gil received a sizable raise from team owner Walter O'Malley.

The Dodgers entered the 1951 season confident that they would make it all the way to the top. They jumped out to a commanding lead over the second-place New York Giants. The cross-town rivalry between these two teams was the most bitter in baseball. As late as August 11th the Dodgers were 13½ games ahead of the stumbling Giants. It seemed certain that Brooklyn would win the league pennant. The Dodger stars had had an outstanding year, and fans were already looking forward to the World Series against the Dodgers' other cross-town rivals, the Yankees.

Late in August, however, the Giants began to gain ground on the Dodgers, and they won 37 of their final 44 games. Meanwhile, the Dodgers began to lose. They began looking over their shoulders, growing more and more worried over the Giants' surprising rally. They had been so far ahead all season that they thought the pennant was won.

On paper the Dodgers were far superior. Hodges finished the season with 40 home runs, 103 RBI's and a .268 batting average. Robinson batted .338. Campa-

nella hit .325, drove in 108 runs and hit 33 homers.
Snider batted in 101 runs and had 29 homers.

But the Dodgers could not shake the Giants, and
with two games to be played in the season, the teams
were tied. The Giants won their remaining two
games. The Dodgers won one game but almost lost the
pennant in the last game of the regular schedule,
against Philadelphia. Jackie Robinson was the hero of
that game, making a fantastic diving catch of a line
drive with the bases loaded in the twelfth inning. Then
in the 14th, he hit a home run to give the Dodgers a
9-8 victory and a tie with the Giants.

According to National League rules, the Giants and
Dodgers had to play a best-of-three playoff series to decide the pennant race. The Giants won the first game
3-1, but the Dodgers came snarling back to take the
second 10-0.

In the final pennant-deciding contest, the Dodgers
took a 4-1 lead, scoring three times in the eighth inning. The Giants failed to score in the bottom of the
eighth and the Dodgers were only three outs from a
World Series date with the Yankees.

"It's hard to remember exactly how I felt in that
ninth inning as we took the field," Hodges said years
later. "All I can recall was a sense of confidence. We
had big Don Newcombe pitching, and he was as strong
as when he started the game. I was sure we'd win."

But Alvin Dark opened the Giants' ninth with a single, and another by Don Mueller sent Dark to third.
After Monte Irvin popped out, Whitey Lockman
slashed a double to left, scoring Dark. Now it was 4-2.

The next batter, outfielder Bobby Thomson, represented the winning run.

At this point Chuck Dressen, the Dodgers' manager, took Newcombe out of the game. Newk objected strongly, but Dressen insisted. Dressen called on Ralph Branca, a right-hander, to pitch in relief. The first pitch was a called strike. Branca delivered again, and Thomson tore into the ball. The Dodger left fielder watched helplessly as it disappeared into the stands. Thomson scarcely touched home, giving the Giants a 5-4 victory, before he was mobbed by Giant players and fans. The game and the season were over, and the Giants were headed for the World Series.

The Dodgers were left in a state of shock. Hodges remembers seeing Branca sitting in the dressing room, crying. He remembers wanting to cry, too. No one said a word. "I must admit it took a long time to forget," Gil said later. "I'm not sure it's something I'll ever completely forget. One minute we were ready for the World Series and the next we were spectators. It was a crushing disappointment."

But soon there was another season to be played, and in 1952 the Dodgers finished four games ahead of the Giants to win the pennant. Hodges had a very productive year, contributing 32 home runs and 102 RBI's while committing only eleven errors in 1,322 fielding chances.

The Dodgers had high hopes that this year they would finally beat the Yankees in the World Series. They had lost the Series to the Yanks in 1947 and 1949, and they wanted revenge. They won the first game and later went ahead of the Yanks, three games to two. But New York won the last two games and the Series. The biggest disappointment was Hodges. In that Series he came to bat 21 times and did not get a hit.

"I suppose I'll always remember that Series," Hodges said. "I didn't know what to do. I had hit well all season, but I just couldn't buy a hit against the Yankees. I felt as though I had personally been responsible for us losing to the Yankees." He later added that remembering his dismal performance helped keep him from being too proud of other accomplishments. "Going hitless in 21 trips to the plate in a World Series will chase away anyone's idea of being a hero," he said.

The slump carried over into the beginning of the 1953 season, and Dodger fans were concerned. One Sunday in May, the Rev. Herbert Redmond was about to deliver a sermon to his congregation in Brooklyn. But he saw that his listeners were uncomfortably warm, so he simply said, "It's far too hot for a sermon. Keep the Commandments—and say a prayer for Gil Hodges."

Hodges pulled out of the slump. He hit over .300 for the first time in his career, drove in 122 runs and hit 31 homers. The Dodgers were spectacular; five of their eight starters batted above .300 and they won the pennant by 13 games. The only sad note was that they lost the World Series to the Yankees again, this time in six games.

Hodges was established as a star on a great team. He was a gentle man, seldom moved to the point of anger.

In 1970 Hodges chats with his former manager Leo Durocher. Durocher's Cubs and Hodges' Mets were fighting for the pennant.

He often took the part of peacemaker during squabbles both on and off the field. Gil played under four managers—Leo Durocher, Burt Shotton, Dressen and Walter Alston—and it was his gentleness that impressed each of them.

"I never saw Gil when he was not poised and in control of himself," said Leo Durocher, who managed the Dodgers in the 1940s. "I almost never saw him get dangerously excited or angry. He was always calm, always determined to do his job. He never gave up when we were far behind, either, which I consider to be the mark of a true professional.

"Just once did I see him get angry. It was during a fight that was touched off when some team's pitcher began throwing at our hitters. Finally, somebody ran out to the mound and it started. It broke out into a free-for-all and suddenly there went Gil, wading through people right into the middle of the commotion. He picked up one guy and threw him. I really mean he threw him. Then he did it to another one, threw him after the first. He ended that thing quickly, because everybody stopped to watch him. They were amazed that he had finally lost his cool. Also, I guess, no one wanted to be next. We all knew how strong he was."

Another side of Hodges which was seldom seen in public was his dry humor. During a game in 1953, Pee Wee Reese received a nasty spike wound trying to make the pivot throw to first. After the game he was up on the trainer's table, receiving first aid for the injury.

Gil walked over and inspected the wound. Then he said, "Pee Wee, why haven't you learned to make that play yet? I just don't understand it. How could you be so foolish as to let yourself get spiked?"

Reese didn't realize that Gil was joking and told him to mind his own business.

Gil continued with a straight face: "Not being able to play without getting spiked is an interesting weakness. What would you say accounts for it—poor reflexes or a lack of intelligence?"

Pee Wee began to yell angrily at Hodges, and Gil

burst out laughing. Reese realized that he had been fooled into losing his temper. He grinned sheepishly and told the first baseman to go soak his head.

Hodges' great play interested many other teams. The most impressive offer the Dodgers received was from Gussie Busch, a brewery owner who also owned the St. Louis Cardinals. Busch asked Eddie Stanky, the Cardinal manager and a former infielder for the Dodgers and Giants, what he needed to insure a Cardinal pennant in 1954. Stanky replied that he needed a hard-hitting first baseman who was a good enough fielder to hold the Cardinal infield together. There was only one man like that—Gil Hodges.

Busch called Dodger owner Walter O'Malley himself. "We need Gil Hodges," he said. "Will you take $175,000 for him?"

O'Malley laughed. "I wouldn't take $600,000," he said. "Are you prepared to go any higher than that? It would be a temptation, but even for a million I'd have to turn it down, I think. The fans of Brooklyn would lynch me if I traded Gil."

The Dodgers lost the pennant in 1954, but in 1955 they won it again and faced the New York Yankees in the World Series for the second time in three years. After losing the first two games, the Dodgers stormed back to win three in a row. The Yanks won the sixth game to tie the Series at three games apiece. Once again the Dodgers had their backs to the wall.

But this time the ending was different. The Dodgers won the seventh game 2-0 and claimed the first World Championship in their history. Young Johnny Podres allowed the Yanks only eight hits and Gil Hodges drove in both Dodger runs. Sandy Amoros, a substitute outfielder, saved the game for Brooklyn with a spectacular catch in the outfield in the sixth inning. Hodges and Brooklyn were finally winners.

The Dodgers beat out the Milwaukee Braves for the pennant in 1956. The Yankees and the Dodgers faced each other again in the World Series and this time the Yanks got revenge for their loss in 1955, defeating the Dodgers in seven games. Hodges had his best Series to date, however, batting .304 and driving in eight runs.

Then after the 1956 season, the Dodgers announced that they would be moving the team from Brooklyn to Los Angeles. Hodges and his teammates were shocked and upset. "I cried when I heard the news," Hodges said, "and my wife cried too. We had grown to love Brooklyn. We still live there today. But I promised Mr. O'Malley I would go to California, and I did."

Despite his disappointment, Hodges still had some good seasons left. In 1959 Gil played on his last pennant-winning team, hitting .276 and leading the Dodgers in home runs with 25. He finished third on the team in runs-batted-in and doubles, and won another fielding championship with only eight errors in 961 chances.

The new Los Angeles fans came to appreciate Gil's play almost as much as the old fans in Brooklyn. He played with injuries and pain, but he never complained. And he contributed mightily with his bat and glove in the tight pennant race near the end of the season. On September 25th he hit a home run in the eleventh inning to beat the Chicago Cubs, allowing the Dodgers to take over first place from the Milwaukee Braves. On the last day of the season the Braves pulled even again and the two teams were tied for the pennant.

For the second time in his career, Hodges was part of a National League playoff series. This time Gil took charge. He produced the tying run in the first game with an eighth-inning double, and the Dodgers went on to win. Then he hit three singles and scored the winning run the next day when Los Angeles took the second game and the pennant. The Dodgers beat the Chicago White Sox in six games in the World Series and Gil contributed nine hits for a lofty .391 Series batting average.

In 1960 and 1961, his final two seasons with the Dodgers, Gil held on to his first-base job, but his hitting began to weaken. "I don't know if the pitchers were getting better or if I was getting older," he said later.

In the winter of 1962 the newly-formed New York Mets were allowed to claim players from other teams and they drafted Gil from the Dodgers. The New York fans remembered him and came to cheer him, but he played in only 54 games. Still, he hit nine home runs in 127 at-bats. He played only eleven games for the Mets in 1963 when he was suddenly called to become manager of the Washington Senators.

"Gil was perfect for the team we had in Washington," explained George Selkirk, the Senators' general manager. "It was a young team, not a very good team, in a league that had some very strong clubs. Naturally, we knew it would be a difficult season. Many other men would have lost their patience, would have pressed for victories and would have ruined the confidence of the young players by benching them. But Gil was like their father. He helped them with their hitting and he acted as a counselor when they had personal problems."

In each of Hodges' five seasons as the Senators' manager, the team improved its record. In his final season, 1967, they won 76 games and finished sixth of ten teams.

Then in the winter of 1968, the New York Mets asked Gil to return—as their manager. Gil quickly accepted. He became the Mets' fourth manager since 1962 and inherited a team that had never finished higher than ninth place.

"This is not a bad team," he said. "It is a young team, and it can win. My job is to get the most out of the players, to teach them how to be winners."

The Mets were ninth again in 1968, but a definite improvement had been made. Gil had uncovered budding young stars, men such as Cleon Jones, Tom Seaver, Bud Harrelson and Ken Boswell. During the season Gil suffered a mild heart attack and spent part of the season away from the ballpark. Fans wondered if he would still be able to manage.

But in the spring of 1969 he was ready to go again. "I don't want to say we can win the pennant," he said. "I know how silly that would sound. But we really could, you know. We really, truly could."

No one believed Gil, but he was right: the amazing Mets finished first in their division, then swept the

Hodges slides into third ahead of the ball during the 1959 World Series against the Chicago White Sox.

Atlanta Braves in three games for the National League pennant. Then they beat the proud Baltimore Orioles in the World Series in five games.

Hodges never lost his poise. "We can win," he said in the frantic September drive, "if we just keep doing things our way. We have the pitching and the defense. There is no reason to suspect that we'll blow it now." He was a unanimous choice for Manager of the Year.

Hodges' new recognition as a manager was only an addition to the recognition he had already received as a player. He was perhaps the finest first baseman, as a hitter and a fielder, in the past 30 years. "If you want the perfect first baseman," said Walt Alston, the long-time manager of the Dodgers, "you would be honor-bound to choose Gil Hodges. He'll go down as one of the best of all time."

BOOG POWELL and WILLIE McCOVEY

Who was the best first baseman of recent years? Some say Boog Powell and others say Willie McCovey. Both were powerful sluggers and good fielders. Both played for championship teams and both became almost automatic All-Star selections. It would be difficult to choose between them.

Boog Powell, the star first baseman of the Baltimore Orioles, didn't begin like a star. He made a decision that cost him $40,000 because of his lackluster play. While playing at Key West High School, Boog attracted several baseball scouts. "I think there were guys talking to me from about fifteen teams," he said years later, "and the highest bonus offer I received was for $65,000." But the scouts wanted Boog to sign right away before the finals of the Florida State Baseball Tournament. If he signed, he would be ineligible to play. "I didn't want to take off and leave my teammates in the middle of the tournament," Boog said. "They were all counting on me, and they were all my friends. I wouldn't have felt right."

So Boog delayed the scouts and played in the tournament. "As it turned out," he joked, "I might as well have signed for all the good I did my team. I got just one single in thirteen times up and most of the scouts figured they had saved their teams a lot of money. Only the Cardinals and the Orioles stayed around after that performance."

Boog and his dad finally agreed to the Orioles' offer of $25,000. It turned out to be one of the best bargains Baltimore ever made.

In 1970, after leading the powerful Orioles to another American League pennant and an easy World Series victory over the Cincinnati Reds, Boog was named the league's Most Valuable Player. He batted .297, with 35 home runs and 114 RBI's while making only ten errors in 1,308 chances in the field. In the World Series he hit .294, hit two home runs and drove in five runs. He was errorless in 38 fielding chances.

Powell's greatest ability was always to terrify American League pitchers. Sam McDowell, who pitched for Cleveland from 1961 to 1971, once tried to explain what it felt like pitching against the powerful Baltimore batting order, which then included Frank Robin-

Boog Powell seems to have his eyes closed as he follows through on a mighty swing.

son, Brooks Robinson, Paul Blair and Dave Johnson.

"There isn't a line-up in the league as strong as that
one," said the Indians' fast-balling left-hander. "I
mean, it's kind of scary. You get rid of one guy and
then up comes another one, and if you get past him all
of a sudden this telephone pole steps up—Boog Powell.
I never want to see him when I'm pitching, but you
know he's there and somehow you have to do something about him. Like pray."

Powell's size alone was enough to frighten pitchers.
He was 6-foot-5 and he weighed "almost anything"—
up to 265 pounds. "When I was fifteen years old I
weighed two hundred and thirty pounds," he said.
"When I got to the major leagues I was around two
hundred and forty. Last year [1970] I played at two-
sixty-five, although I didn't say anything about it to our
manager. I just knew he would think it was too heavy,
but I didn't consider myself fat at all. I never felt slow.
I didn't get tired. I am just a big guy, and I can't do
anything about it. I take care of myself and I stay in
shape."

Boog's size led many people to think he could not
field. "People figure because I'm so big I can't be a
good fielder," he said. "Well, that's wrong. I love to
field. It's a challenge. I think I handle more than my
share of tough grounders, and I help out our infielders
by saving more of their bad throws. I guess I'm a
pretty big target for them, right? It's kind of hard to
miss me."

John Wesley Powell was born August 17, 1941, in

Lakeland, Florida. In 1953, when Boog was twelve, he played on the Lakeland Little League team with his brother Charley and his step-brother, Carl Taylor. The team was so good that it advanced all the way to the Little League World Series in Williamsport, Pennsylvania. Boog pitched, Carl caught and Charley played in the outfield.

The game that Boog pitched was a disaster. "I gave up fifteen runs in the first three innings," he recalled with a frown. "We lost 16-0. But I did hit a long double off the wall."

When Boog was 14, the Powells moved to Key West, where Boog and his brothers joined the Pony League team. George Mira, who later became an NFL quarterback, did the pitching and Boog moved to the outfield. The team went all the way to the national finals of the Pony League Tournament before losing to Rome, Georgia.

When Boog was a high school senior, many colleges offered him basketball and football scholarships, but he chose baseball and the Orioles. Baltimore sent him to the minor league team in Bluefield, West Virginia, in the Appalachian League. There he hit .351, drove in 59 runs and set a league record with 15 home runs. He spent that winter in a Florida Instructional League camp, where he worked on his fielding. "Nobody ever worked harder on grounders," said a scout who was there. "By the time that camp was done, he was a good fielding first baseman."

In 1960 Boog played at Appleton, Wisconsin, where his manager was Earl Weaver. Weaver was also moving up toward the major leagues, and he arrived as manager of the Orioles in 1968. Boog climbed to Triple-A ball in 1961, playing for Rochester of the International League. He hit .321, collecting 32 homers and driving in 92 runs and leading the league in hits (156) and total bases (288).

But another problem entered his life that summer. Since the Orioles had a veteran first baseman named Jim Gentile, they decided Boog would have a better chance if he played the outfield. So he spent the winter of 1961–62 in the Florida Instructional League, this time learning to be a left fielder.

"I always had trouble judging fly balls," he said with a smile, "but what I got to, I held on to. And I never made mistakes like throwing to the wrong base or the cutoff man. Still, I liked first base much better."

Boog made it to the Orioles in 1962, where he played mostly in left field. He had trouble hitting left-handed pitchers, and for two seasons he was platooned, playing only against right-handed pitchers. Powell got off on the wrong foot against left-handers. Whitey Ford, a star lefty for the New York Yankees, was responsible. "When I was a rookie," Powell said, "my first game was against New York, and Ford was pitching. I think he threw me nine curve balls and I struck out three times. But that man was great. He's the finest pitcher I ever had to face."

In 1964 Boog finally reached his star potential. He slammed 39 home runs, drove in 99 runs and batted .290. He weighed 255 pounds that season, 15 pounds more than the team's maximum playing weight, but he had such a good year that he earned a bonus anyway.

Then in 1965 Boog suffered through the first of a series of mysterious slumps. In one string in July he came to bat 32 times without a hit. His average for the season dropped to .248 and he hit only 17 homers.

That same year, Powell had a disagreement with the Orioles' manager Hank Bauer. "He made me get on the scale in August," Boog recalled, "and I weighed two-fifty-one. Hank decided I wasn't hitting because I was too heavy. So he ordered me to lose ten pounds in ten days or be fined. I got down to two-forty-three, but he fined me anyway. I thought it was cheap and unfair, and we had a dandy run-in. But I always had a lot of respect for Hank. I think he was just upset over the team losing."

Boog spent the winter fishing—his favorite pastime —and reported in 1966 with renewed confidence. "I just can't explain the slumps I get into," he says, "but man, when I'm into one, it seems like forever until I break out."

During the winter, the Orioles were able to make a major trade, sending three players to Cincinnati for Frank Robinson. Robinson had been an established star and a Most Valuable Player at Cincinnati. He was stung by the trade and by the Cincinnati claim that he was "over the hill." Robinson was determined to make 1966 his best year ever. Powell was determined, too. He wanted to make up for his 1965 slump.

The two of them enjoyed a super season. Robinson won the American League's Most Valuable Player

Baltimore's big guns, Powell, Brooks Robinson and Frank Robinson, smile after clinching the pennant in 1966.

award and the Triple Crown, leading the league in batting average (.316), home runs (49) and RBI's (122). Boog hit .287 and had 34 homers and 109 RBI's. He was named Comeback Player of the Year. Best of all, the Orioles, who had been third-place finishers two seasons in a row, won the American League pennant by nine games. In the World Series, the Orioles overpowered the Los Angeles Dodgers, winning in four straight games against such pitchers as Sandy Koufax and Don Drysdale. Boog hit .357 in the Series.

In the next two seasons Boog fell victim to his

strange slumps again. He began to worry about being traded and about losing his big salary. "I just didn't know how to explain it," he said, "but I knew I had to do something. I spent the winter of 1968 running and running and running. I had to get myself into the best shape of my life, because I knew another bad season in 1969 might end my career."

Boog made it all the way back. He hit .304 in 1969, the first time he had ever gone over the .300 mark in the major leagues. He drove in 121 runs and slammed 37 home runs. The Orioles won another pennant, but lost to the New York Mets in the World Series.

Powell continued to shine in 1970, helping the Orioles to their second straight pennant. "Now I have confidence," he said. "And I'm getting a sense of responsibility toward the team. I found myself taking more time at the plate, not swinging at everything. I made notes on certain pitchers and certain parks. I stopped trying to pull everything to right field. I just couldn't afford to have any more of those bad years. Neither could the team."

Boog hit two home runs against Cincinnati in the 1970 World Series, drove in five runs and hit .294. Then in 1971 he slipped back again, hitting only .256. The Orioles continued their winning ways, however, winning another division title and defeating Oakland in three straight games for the pennant. In the World Series, though, the Pittsburgh Pirate pitchers handcuffed Powell and the Orioles, winning the Series in seven games.

After the season Frank Robinson was traded to the

Powell tags the A's Bert Campaneris on a pick-off play during the 1971 season.

Dodgers. But the Baltimore line-up was still intimidating. With Boog Powell waiting for good pitches and Brooks Robinson waiting for his, what could the American League pitchers do?

"Pray," said Sam McDowell. "Just pray he doesn't tag one."

Willie Lee McCovey almost gave up athletics when he was growing up in Mobile, Alabama. "There were eight brothers and two sisters in my family," he recalled, "but I was the only one who played baseball, or any other sport. A couple of my brothers boxed in the Golden Gloves for a while, but I was the only one who liked team sports. Man, I played 'em all, but it was kind of difficult, I guess. Even my father had no interest in sports, and I used to wonder if something was wrong with me, always playing games.

"But there wasn't much else for a kid to do in Mobile. I started out on the playgrounds as a kid, mostly playing basketball. Then I went on to football and baseball. By the time I got to high school, I was able to make all the teams. I always thought my best sport was basketball, but since I hurt my knees I haven't played much of that. I'm sure glad I still had baseball."

Baseball fans were glad, too. Willie soon became the strapping 6-foot-4, 220-pound first baseman for the San Francisco Giants. The fans called him "Stretch" for the way he could reach for wide throws at first base or "Big Bopper" for the way he could hit the ball. Whatever his nickname, he was soon one of the Giants' Big Three along with Willie Mays and Juan Marichal.

Willie was born in Mobile on January 10, 1938. He first gained attention as an athlete at Mobile Central High School where he won three letters in each of the three major sports—baseball, basketball and football. Although several major league teams had shown interest in him, Willie signed with the Giants (who then played in New York) when he graduated in 1955. He spent his first season in Sandersville of the Georgia

State League and immediately gained a reputation as a slugger. He hit 19 homers, drove in 113 runs and batted .305.

He was moved to Danville of the Carolina League in 1956 and to Dallas of the Texas League in 1957. With Dallas he suffered a knee injury which bothered him throughout his career.

"We were playing a night game in Fort Worth and I was on third base when the next guy up hit a slow grounder," he recalled later. "I thought I could score, so I took off and slid into home. I hit hard, and I felt pain in my knee. For a long time I had trouble running."

Willie had torn some cartilage in his right knee, and two years later he was forced to have an operation to repair the injury. From then on, the knee required constant exercise and conditioning each year. Years later, when he was a major-league veteran, he said, "I spend most of each winter lifting weights with that knee to keep it strong and flexible. But I have developed arthritis there and that means more problems. It does bother me, but I won't complain about it. I love to play this game too much. A hard infield always makes it more painful, because all the impact travels right up my leg to the knee."

The only real problem resulting from the damaged knee was a loss of speed. "Believe it or not," McCovey said later, "I was very fast. When I first joined the Giants' organization, I was timed as the fastest player in our whole minor league camp in the hundred-yard dash. I think I ran it in ten seconds flat."

Willie spent two seasons with Phoenix of the Pacific Coast League before he made it to the Giants in the middle of the 1959 season. "My first major league game was July 30, 1959," he once recalled, a broad smile on his face. "I had four hits. It tied a major-league record." He went on to be named the National League's Rookie of the Year. In 52 games he hit .354 and slammed 13 home runs.

Willie spent 17 games the next season in Tacoma getting back in shape after his knee operation. Then he returned to the Giants to stay. But making it to the

Rookie Willie McCovey in 1959.

Giants was only part of the battle, for the Giants had Orlando Cepeda, a fine power-hitting first baseman, who had been named Rookie of the Year in 1958.

For the next three years (1960–1962), Willie shared first base duties with Cepeda. Although his hitting improved, he appeared in only about half of the Giant games. In 1963 the Giants decided that McCovey was too valuable to have on the bench and he became a regular in the outfield. Then in 1965 Cepeda suffered a serious knee injury and Willie returned to his first base post. The following year Cepeda was traded to the St. Louis Cardinals.

The 1962 season was a big one for the Giants. They ended the regular season tied with the Los Angeles Dodgers. In the three-game playoff to decide the winner of the pennant, each team won one of the first two games. Willie once said that the final game of the playoff was "the most dramatic game I've ever played in." The Giants were behind by two runs when Dodger relief pitcher Stan Williams came in to pitch to McCovey in the ninth. Willie walked and then scored on Willie Mays' home run. Then Williams loaded the bases and walked in the winning run.

"I think I felt a little sorry for Williams," said McCovey. "He was a good pitcher but he had all that pressure on him. I didn't get to feelin' too sorry, though. After all, it did get us into the World Series."

In that Series the Giants faced the New York Yankees. The teams traded victories until they had won three apiece. In the seventh game Willie was almost the hero. In the ninth inning the Giants were behind by a 1-0 score when McCovey came to the plate with two men on base and two out. Ralph Terry, the Yankees' pitcher, worked the count to one ball and one strike. Then Willie lashed out at a high fast ball. It was a vicious line drive and it seemed sure to go for extra bases. But Bobby Richardson, the Yankees' second baseman, leaped and made a desperate one-handed stab for the ball. It stuck in the webbing of his glove, and the Series was over.

"I always felt that was the hardest I ever hit a ball," Willie said later. "I was very excited when I felt it go. I would have bet anything it was going to be a hit. But you can't take anything away from Richardson. He made a super play. The ball should have been at least a double, and I think it would have been enough to win the game, but he caught it. If it had been another inch higher, he just wouldn't have reached it. Now I know why they say baseball is a game of inches. Just one more inch and we would have won the World Series."

The 1963 season was Willie's first as a regular starter. His 44 home runs led the major leagues, and he had a .280 batting average and 102 RBI's. Along with Willie Mays, Cepeda and Felipe Alou, Willie helped make the Giant line-up the most feared in the majors, but the Giants finished third.

Beginning in 1965 when McCovey became the regular Giant first baseman, the combination of McCovey on first and Mays in center field triggered the Giants' offense. In the next six years McCovey registered home run totals of 39, 36, 31, 36, 45 and 39, leading the league twice. He drove in more than 100 runs

"Stretch" McCovey takes a throw to put out the Pirates' Vic Davalillo by inches in 1971.

three years in a row. He compiled 370 home runs through the 1971 season and played in six All-Star games. In 1969 he was voted the National League's Most Valuable Player, with 45 homers, 126 RBI's and a .320 average.

"I don't find any pitcher who can always get me out," he said. "Sure, a few have given me a lot of trouble. Sandy Koufax was one. But no pitcher scares me. Every team has three or four who can be very tough on a given day, but I have enough confidence. I believe I can hit any pitcher.

"Guys I've never faced before, young kids, cause me the most trouble," he continued. "I learn the veterans and I can figure out what they'll do. But the younger ones are different. I don't know what they'll throw when they're behind on the count. I don't know whether it's that the kids are stronger or that the overall quality of pitching is tougher, but it seems harder to hit now than it did when I first came up."

Willie's big disappointment in the major leagues has been that he played in only one World Series. "It must mean I haven't contributed enough," he said in 1970. "Because, Lord knows, we've been close often enough. We've been second three times and third three times. I've never been able to stay over .300, and maybe that's my problem. Maybe if I hit for a higher average, the team would win more. I think I'm capable of the .280 to .290 seasons, and maybe once in a while I'll get up over .300. That's my limit, I guess, and I'm stuck with it."

But if Willie was "stuck" with his capabilities, so

were the pitchers who faced him. As pitcher Whitey Ford once said, "Guys who hit .300 aren't going to smack your best pitch seven miles out of the park. Guys like McCovey scare me to death. I would rather pitch to a singles hitter with a .300 batting average."

McCovey's frustration reached a new high point in 1971. The Giants started the season strongly, but Willie was handicapped all year by a new knee injury. He batted .277 and hit only 18 home runs. The Giants gave up a big lead to the Los Angeles Dodgers late in the season and the race for the Western Division title went down to the last day of the season. Juan Marichal pitched a five-hitter to give the Giants a 5-1 victory over San Diego and their first first-place finish since 1962.

The Giants faced the Pittsburgh Pirates in the divisional playoffs for the National League pennant. In the first game McCovey hit a long home run in the fifth inning to give the Giants a 5-1 lead, and they beat the Pirates 5-4. But the Pirates came back to take the next two games and needed only one more win for the pennant. In the fourth game Willie drove in the first Giant run in the first inning. Then he came to bat in the second with the score tied 2-2 and two men on base. Another long homer gave the Giants a 5-2 lead. But Pittsburgh came back with seven runs to win the game and the pennant. The Giants and Willie McCovey had been stopped again just short of the World Series. Willie had slammed six hits in 14 at-bats in the playoffs and driven in six of the Giants' 15 runs.

After the 1971 season Willie faced more knee surgery. At the age of 34 he did not look forward to the surgery and the long recovery time it would require. But if the knee could be repaired, Willie said, he planned to play until he was at least 40. National League pitchers hoped for his recovery but didn't look forward to his return to the Giant line-up.

JACKIE ROBINSON

Today one player out of three in the major leagues is black, and many of the greatest stars of recent years are black—Willie Mays, Hank Aaron, Frank Robinson and many others. But in 1946 there had not been a Negro player in the major leagues for nearly 50 years.

Most team owners and many players and fans felt that blacks should be kept out of professional baseball. In those days Negroes went to separate schools and sat in separate sections on buses and in theaters. If they played baseball, they played in separate Negro leagues. There was no written rule that said a black man could not play in the majors, but there was an unwritten agreement never to hire one.

Jackie Robinson was the first black man to play in the major leagues in modern times. He had to be a strong hitter and a good fielder—much better than average. But he also had to be much more. He had to be able to smile at insults and ignore the taunts of a crowd. He had to play well even when he was being treated badly by players and fans alike. He would be the only black man among more than 400 major-league players.

The man who brought Jackie to the major leagues was Branch Rickey, the president of the Brooklyn Dodgers. Rickey believed that the "color line" in baseball should be broken, and he knew that there were many black players who were good enough to play in the major leagues. But he also knew that the first black man to play in the majors would have to be extraordinary. Rickey ordered the Dodger scouts to look for such a man. They soon found him, playing for the Kansas City Monarchs, one of the best teams in the Negro leagues.

Rickey sent for Robinson and explained what he planned to do. If Jackie was willing to try, he would play one year for the Montreal Royals, the Dodgers' top minor league club. Then if he succeeded, he would play second base for the Brooklyn Dodgers. Jackie agreed.

On October 23, 1945, Hector Racine, president of the Montreal Royals, called a press conference. There he introduced Jackie Robinson to the baseball writers. "Gentlemen," he said, "this is Jackie Robinson. He has just been signed to play for the Montreal club for the 1946 season."

The news spread quickly. It was clear that Branch Rickey was planning to bring the young infielder into the majors. When the 1946 season opened, the baseball world watched Robinson closely to see if the first black man in organized baseball could make the grade at Montreal. Jackie responded magnificently. He led the league in batting with a .349 average and tied for the lead in runs scored with 113. He stole 40 bases and led all second basemen in fielding with a .985 mark. The Royals won the pennant and went on to the Little World Series against Louisville. Jackie was booed by the Louisville fans but he led his team to the championship, batting .333 and scoring the winning run in the final game.

The fans at Montreal treated Robinson as a hero. He liked Montreal and later told a newspaper man that he liked Montreal so well he would have been willing to stay there.

But Rickey was determined. He called for Robinson and told him he would be playing for the Dodgers that spring—if he could take it. "Are you man enough to take what they're going to give you?" he demanded. "Do you have the guts to take it all?"

"I've got the guts," Robinson answered angrily. "I fight for my rights. I won't let any man walk all over me."

"That's wrong," Rickey said. "Did you ever think it takes more guts to be abused and not fight back? They'll try to make you fight. They'll turn this game into a riot if you let them. They'll spike you and they'll throw at you and they'll call you every dirty name there is. They'll insult you and your wife and your parents, and I don't want you to do a thing. You've got to prove yourself with your bat and your glove and your speed. Nothing more. You must play clean baseball, hard but clean. You've got to learn to be deaf and unfeeling. You've got to learn to take it."

Robinson sat for a moment, "All right," he said, "I understand. I'll take it. I'll learn to ignore them. I'll turn the other cheek. And I'll prove I can be the best player in the major leagues."

Rickey smiled. The final arrangements for breaking the color line had been made. Now it was all up to Jackie Robinson.

Jackie Robinson confers with Dodger President Branch Rickey.

Before he appeared in his first game Jackie faced another challenge. The Dodgers had a good veteran second baseman named Eddie Stanky. They wanted Jackie to play first base. All through spring training he worked at learning a new position. But when the season opened he was ready. He played 151 games, hit .297, drove in 48 runs, stole 29 bases and belted a dozen home runs.

The Dodgers won the National League pennant in 1947, and their young first baseman was acclaimed as the National League's Rookie of the Year. In the World Series against the New York Yankees, Robinson stole two bases and collected seven hits, but the Dodgers lost in seven games.

There were many new faces on the 1948 Dodger team. Gil Hodges became the regular first baseman. Stanky was traded and Robinson took over second. Billy Cox was the new third baseman and Roy Campanella, also a Negro, was the rookie catcher. A young outfielder named Duke Snider was also beginning to play.

In the spring of 1948 Jackie had a problem with his weight. "I'm hog fat," he said bitterly. "I didn't take care of myself." Leo Durocher, the Dodgers' manager, was enraged. "I'll work Robinson at second base all during spring training," he said. "The only way to get that blubber off his belly is to get him so tired he'll wish he never heard of me or baseball."

The rapid weight loss affected Robinson's speed and strength, and he said he was displeased with his 1948 performance. Still, he hit .296, led all second basemen in fielding with a .980 average, stole 22 bases, drove in 85 runs and hit twelve homers. The young Dodgers finished third.

By 1949 Jackie was changing. No longer was he the polite, turn-the-other-cheek Negro player. He became more confident and sure of himself, and his natural competitiveness showed itself more and more.

"They'd better be careful of me now," he said. "I'm going to be rough on everybody this season."

It was a marvelous season. He ran the bases with reckless abandon, challenging every pitcher in the league and stealing 37 bases. He made spectacular fielding plays, turning apparent hits into outs. And he hit the ball consistently, leading the league with a .342 average. He also slammed 16 home runs, drove in 124 runs and scored 122 runs. Jackie was chosen Most Valuable Player in the National League by a near-unanimous vote. He was 30 years old, but it was only his third season in the league. The Dodgers won the pennant in the National League but lost again to the Yankees in the World Series.

"That year, more than any other year in my career, my hits counted," Jackie recalled later. "It seemed as though every time I came up with runners in scoring position I was confident I would get them home. Most of the time I did. It was also a glorious year because I enjoyed good health and I avoided injuries. And for the first time, I really stopped thinking about being black. I was part of a team, and there were a few other Negroes in the majors, and most of the bad experiences had stopped. I will always remember that year as the

Robinson steals home safely against the Phillies during the tight 1950 pennant race. Batter Gil Hodges watches.

season I enjoyed most in the major leagues."

Jackie played with almost equal brilliance in 1950. He hit .328, drove in 81 runs, scored 99 and hit 14 homers. Meanwhile, the Dodgers were involved in one of the most dramatic pennant races in baseball history. The Philadelphia Phillies caught fire in mid-May and moved from fifth place to take over the league lead in July. With twelve games remaining in the season the Phillies held a nine-game lead. They seemed to be out of danger.

But the Dodgers refused to give up, and paced by the fiery Robinson, they maintained a steady pressure. Slowly the lead was reduced, until the Dodgers beat the Phillies on September 30, cutting their lead to one game. If the Dodgers could beat the Phillies on the last day of the season, they would tie for the league lead and force a three-game playoff for the pennant.

The game was played on a Sunday afternoon in Brooklyn, and the stadium was packed to capacity. Roy Campanella remembered the excitement years later. "They were swingin' from the rafters and sittin' next to us on the bench," he joked. "I never saw so many people in one place."

The game entered the ninth inning tied at 1-1. The Phillies went down without a score. The Dodgers came up and Cal Abrams, an outfielder, drew a walk. Pee Wee Reese singled to left, putting men on first and second. Then Duke Snider, the powerful center fielder, came up. He lined a single over second. Abrams made the turn at third and dashed for home. Richie Ashburn, Philadelphia's center fielder, threw to the plate, and Abrams, who had taken too wide a turn at third, was out by 15 feet. Robinson came up in this dramatic situation, but was given an intentional walk, loading the bases. Then Furillo fouled out, and Hodges ended the inning with a long fly to left. In the tenth the Phillies came up with three runs and won the game 4-1. The Dodgers had been beaten.

Then came 1951. The Dodgers won their first ten games and were in first place all season. Almost every player in the line-up was a top performer. Robinson enjoyed a super season, hitting .338, driving in 88 runs, hitting 19 homers, and stealing 25 bases.

On August 11 the second place New York Giants

were 13½ games out. Then they got hot and began chasing the Dodgers. They won 37 of their last 44 games while the Dodgers fell into a slump. On the final day of the season, with the Dodgers playing Philadelphia and the Giants at home against Boston, the two teams were tied.

The Giants won their game 3-2. The Dodgers, meanwhile, were hooked up in a pressure game with the proud Phillies. Philadelphia led 8-5 in the eighth, but Brooklyn got three runs to tie the score.

The ninth was scoreless. So was the tenth and the eleventh. But in the bottom of the twelfth the Phillies loaded the bases with two men out, and the Dodgers were one hit away from being eliminated. The Philadelphia batter was Eddie Waitkus, a solid-hitting first baseman.

Waitkus slammed a low, sinking line drive between the shortstop and the second baseman. It looked like a sure hit, but Jackie Robinson refused to quit. He raced to his right, then dived frantically for the ball, glove-hand extended. He snared the liner just inches off the grass. The score remained tied.

Now it was the fourteenth, and two men were out when Jackie came up. As he told it later his mind was racing at that moment. "Somehow, I knew we were going to do it. We were going to get the run in."

The Phillies' pitcher, Robin Roberts, worked the count to one ball, one strike. Then he offered a fastball, waist high. Jackie swung and knew from the instant he hit it that it was gone. It was a home run, driven deep into the left-field stands. The Phillies couldn't score in

After forcing the runner at second, Robinson fires the ball to Hodges at first for the double play.

the bottom of the inning, and Brooklyn had a 9-8 victory. They had saved a tie with the Giants and now faced their bitter rivals in a three-game playoff for the pennant.

The teams split the first two games. In the third game the Dodgers led 4-2 in the last of the ninth when the Giants' Bobby Thomson hit a three-run homer to win the pennant for the Giants. For the second season in a row the Dodgers had lost the pennant in the last game of the season.

In 1952 Robinson batted .308, hit 19 home runs, drove in 75 runs and stole 24 bases. In addition he led National League second basemen for the fourth year in a row in double plays. Pee Wee Reese, Gil Hodges and Robinson made up one of the great double-play combinations in history. The Dodgers won the 1952 pennant after two years of disappointment. However, they faced the Yankees in the World Series and lost to them for the third time in six years.

In the final four years of his career Jackie hit over .300 twice and continued to spark the Dodgers. Junior Gilliam replaced him at second base, but Robinson alternated between third base and the outfield. The Dodgers won three more pennants, and in 1955 they beat the Yankees in the World Series in seven games.

In Jackie's last season, 1956, the Dodgers again won the National League flag. For the sixth time in his career he would be facing the Yankees in the World Series. The Dodgers had lost the first four, but now they had a chance to win two in a row. Jackie knew that it might be his last Series—although he had not announced it, he was thinking about retiring.

"I had played ten years," he said later, "and I had started late. I was twenty-eight when I was a rookie. I was getting tired, and my muscles were aching. My speed had gone, and my batting eye. But I sure wanted that one more World Series, and I was happy it was going to be against the Yankees again."

With the teams tied at two games apiece, Yankee pitcher Don Larsen beat the Dodgers, throwing the first no-hitter and perfect game ever pitched in a World Series.

The Dodgers had to win the sixth game or lose the Series. When Jackie came up with two men on in the bottom of the tenth inning, neither team had scored and the Dodgers had been held to only three hits. He slammed the ball over the left fielder's head and the winning run scored. As it turned out, it was his last hit in the majors. The next day the Yankees shellacked the Dodgers 9-0 to win the Series, and Robinson went hitless, striking out to end the game.

During the winter of 1956–57 the Dodgers traded Robinson to the New York Giants. Chub Feeney, president of the Giants, called Robinson and asked if he would play. "I'll have to ask for some time to think about it," he said. "I'm just not sure of what I'll do."

Jackie announced his retirement on January 6, 1957, in a story in *Look* magazine. "I am thirty-eight years old, with a family to support," he wrote. "I have to think of my future and about security. At my age, a man doesn't have much future in baseball and very little security."

And so, at 38 years of age, Jackie Robinson left the game he had helped to change. Such outstanding Negro stars as Willie Mays, Hank Aaron, Frank Robinson and Ernie Banks were safely established in the major leagues. Jackie had paved the way for a whole generation of stars.

John Jack Roosevelt Robinson was born January 31, 1919, in Cairo, Georgia. He was one of five children born to Jerry and Mallie Robinson, who were poor tenant farmers. Shortly after Jackie was born his father left the family. Then in 1920 Mallie Robinson moved her family to Pasadena, California, where her brother lived. She found a job as a cleaning woman, doing cooking, washing and ironing, and the Robinson children had to fend for themselves. Jackie's older sister, Willa Mae, took him to school with her when he was only four years old because there was nowhere else for him to stay while his mother worked and his brothers and sisters attended classes.

After Jackie started school, he earned pocket money by watering flowers for neighbors, hauling old papers to the local junkman and shining shoes. He sold hot dogs at the Rose Bowl, caddied at local golf courses and delivered Sunday newspapers.

As Jackie approached his teenage years, sports entered his life. His older brother, Mack, became a track star, running the dash and sprint events. He was good enough to earn a place on the United States track team for the 1936 Olympics. He finished second to Jesse Owens in the 200-meter dash. Jackie admired his brother and said that Mack gave him the incentive to enter sports competition on his own.

"He was really a super athlete," Jackie said. "Sometimes I wonder how much he might have been able to do if he was the youngest, like me, and not concerned with helping to support our family."

Jackie's first love was football, which he learned to play on the sandlots of Pasadena without equipment. When he entered Muir Technical High School he won letters in four sports. But football provided him with his greatest recognition. After high school he decided to continue his education. He enrolled in Pasadena City College. There he set a national junior college broad-jump record with a leap of 25 feet, six and one-third inches, breaking the record that had been set by his brother Mack. After completing his work at the two-year City College, Jackie went on to the University of California at Los Angeles (UCLA) on an athletic scholarship. He earned All-America honors as a football halfback, earned letters in basketball, baseball, track and field, and even boxing. Los Angeles sportswriters claimed that he was the greatest all-round athlete ever to attend UCLA.

In the spring of his senior year Jackie decided to quit school. Although he was near graduation, he felt guilty that his mother and brothers and sisters had to work to support him. He felt he should contribute to the family, too. Less than a year later the U.S. entered World War II, and Jackie was drafted into the army. He became a lieutenant and was discharged in 1945. That spring he took his first job as a professional baseball

A great all-round athlete, Jackie shows his form as a broad-jumper (top) and as a running back for UCLA.

player with the Kansas City Monarchs of the Negro leagues.

Before he had even gotten settled, Robinson discovered that Branch Rickey was interested in him. There was talk that black players would one day play in the major leagues. In October of 1945, Robinson was at the press conference in Montreal where it was announced that he would break the color line in pro baseball.

Sixteen years later, in 1961, Jackie Robinson was elected to baseball's Hall of Fame. In those years he had shown his talent as one of the great second basemen in history. More important, through his courage he had changed the face of baseball.

KEN HUBBS AND GLENN BECKERT

Not every promising player in baseball will be named Most Valuable Player in his league or win a batting or fielding championship. There have been many stories of talented and promising young players whose careers have been cut short by accident or injury. One of the most tragic of these stories is that of Ken Hubbs.

Kenny Hubbs spent two years and ten games as a major leaguer. He came up to the Chicago Cubs at the end of the 1961 season when he was 19 years old. Then in 1962 he became the Cubs' regular second baseman and was named the National League's Rookie

Twenty-year-old Ken Hubbs signs autographs during his errorless streak in 1962.

of the Year. In his first full season he showed talent as a second baseman that has not been seen before or since.

He set two major league records for second basemen. He played 78 consecutive games and handled 418 consecutive chances without an error. No second baseman has done as well since the major leagues began in 1876. He played 159 games at second and his fielding average (.983) was third in the league. At bat he was less spectacular, but he scored 90 runs, batted in 48 and hit .260. He still had much to learn, since he led the league in strikeouts with 129. But for a 20-year-old rookie he was nothing short of spectacular.

In 1963 the Cubs won more games than they lost for the first time since 1949. Hubbs handled 831 chances at second with only 22 errors. He was still having trouble at bat, but he was a promising hitter and he looked forward to a long major-league career. The Cubs were building a pennant contender, and Kenny Hubbs was one of the most promising contributors. The Cubs and their fans were looking forward to 1964.

But when spring training started, Kenny wasn't there. A few days earlier he decided to fly in a private plane from Provo, Utah, to his hometown of Colton, California, to visit his parents. When he had not arrived in Colton by nightfall, airport officials listed him as missing "somewhere between Provo and Colton." Two days later a search party found the wreckage of the small plane. Ken Hubbs was dead.

The Cubs were stunned. "In Ken Hubbs, we had a young star," said an official team statement. "We join his family in their deep mourning, as do all who have had contact with this wonderful young man, tall, handsome, reserved and yet somehow radiant with an inner warmth. His superb skill and courage on the field made him a favorite with the fans and his teammates. At just twenty-two, he seemed on his way to becoming one of baseball's superstars. . . ."

Kenneth Douglass Hubbs was born December 23, 1941, in Riverside, California. When he was still in grade school his family moved to Colton, where he became the local sports legend. He was a man for all seasons, starring in track and field, baseball, basketball and football.

Kenny had stacks of college scholarship offers, but he wanted to be a baseball player. He signed with the Cubs for a $15,000 bonus. Others had received larger bonuses, but Ken didn't care. He wanted the chance to become a professional ballplayer.

For the next three seasons Ken played for a series of Cub farm teams. He played in Mosstown, Tennessee; Fort Worth, Texas; Lancaster, Pennsylvania; and Wenatchee, Oregon. It was at Wenatchee that he found new direction.

Kenny had become bogged down at his position, which was then third base. One day Bobby Adams, a Cubs' scout and coach, visited Wenatchee to find out what was wrong with "that Hubbs kid." Hubbs was promising, but he was not progressing as fast as the Cubs had hoped.

He had become ordinary in the field and was struggling at bat. Adams saw something special. "He could be a great second baseman," he said. "Let's try him there." So they went to work. Kenny was prodded by Adams. "He had me work on the pivot play one hundred times a day," Hubbs once said. "I was doing it in my sleep after a while. But I'll never forget what Mr. Adams did for me. He turned me into a baseball player."

Late in the 1961 season Ken joined the Cubs, playing in ten games. The next year he played second base in all but three games for the Cubs and became

Hubbs charges to his right to make a spectacular play.

Rookie of the Year. The 6-foot-2, 180-pounder was a major league regular before he passed his 21st birthday.

On June 13, playing against the Pirates, he fluffed a ground ball. It was his last error until September 5—78 games and 418 plays later. One veteran newspaperman, who acted as official scorer several times during Kenny's amazing streak, reflected the amazement of writers and fans: "He might not blow another play until the day he trips on his beard. He is a sight to behold fielding a ball or chasing a pop fly. I can't recall any man who was better than this rookie as a fielder. Not in all my years."

When he accepted the award as Rookie of the Year,

Ken was a satisfied young man. "This is like a dream come true," he said. "This is what I have always wanted: baseball."

In 1963, Ken's second full season, the Cubs had a new manager, Bob Kennedy. "In his second year," Kennedy remembered, "the pitchers found a way to hurt him at the plate. He had been punching the outside pitches to right field, and they began to jam him inside. He had to learn how to pull those balls. He was learning well. . . . You'll never know how good he might have been, but I have my own ideas. I think he might have been a Hall of Famer. I think he was that good."

Kenny Hubbs never approached Mickey Mantle's salary or Willie Mays' headlines. He set two major league records in his short career, but he did not have time to make good the promise he showed. Those who saw him play can only talk about his achievements and wonder how great he might have been.

When Ken Hubbs' plane crashed, Glenn Beckert was playing for a Cubs' farm team in Salt Lake City. He had been a minor leaguer since 1962.

"I remember that day," Beckert said later. "We all followed the Cubs' players, and Ken was one of my heroes. But I never thought about playing his position, because I was a shortstop then. And not a very good one, either."

As a shortstop Beckert was not succeeding. His arm wasn't strong enough for the long throws, and when he worried about his fielding, his batting suffered. Glenn had originally signed with the Red Sox but was claimed by the Cubs in the 1962 minor-league draft. They sent him to Wenatchee, where Ken Hubbs had played a few years earlier, and then to Salt Lake City.

But the Chicago scouting department was not impressed. Beckert was quick with his hands, but he didn't get the ball away quickly. He was a fast runner but he didn't run the bases well. He had the chance to be a solid hitter but something kept holding him back.

John Holland, the team's vice president, would not give up on Beckert. "He was aggressive and determined," Holland said. "He was a hustler, a winning type of player. We decided to try him at another position." Glenn was sent to the Cubs' winter instructional league in Florida after the 1964 season. No longer was he a shortstop. He had been given three months to learn how to play second base.

He learned well. "The shorter distance from second to first took care of my weak arm," he said. "I had no trouble at all making those throws. And once I stopped worrying, my hitting came around. I decided I was never going to be a slugger. If I hit a home run once in a while, I'm honestly surprised. So I concentrated on hitting hard grounders, on bunting, on slapping the ball to the opposite field. I didn't want to give up and go home. I still thought I could play."

Glenn had learned determination as a boy. "I grew up in a neighborhood in Pittsburgh where you received recognition through sports," he said. "I was always small. Even through high school, I was smaller than everybody else. I don't think I weighed a hundred and

forty pounds when I graduated. But I still wanted to be
the best. I wanted to be a professional baseball player."

His ambition was postponed for four years, however. Glenn had promised his father he would go to
college, and he did. He earned a degree in political sci-
ence from Allegheny College, near Pittsburgh. There
he met Bob Garback, the Allegheny baseball coach and
a former major leaguer.

"He was inexperienced," Garback recalled later,
"but I saw in him the alertness and the aggressiveness
to make a big leaguer. I worked with him, worked
hard. I felt I owed him whatever help I could offer."

The Red Sox offered Glenn an $8,000 bonus con-
tract, and he grabbed the opportunity. But it remained
for John Holland to find Beckert's true position. Once
that was settled, he went on to become a National
League All-Star.

Beckert spent the 1964 season at Salt Lake City. But
in 1965 he took over as the Cubs' second baseman.
Ernie Banks, the great Cub shortstop and first baseman, later remembered Beckert as a rookie. "When he
first joined the Cubs he was a very quiet kid," Banks
said. "Now he's a holler guy. I don't mean that rah-rah
business. He's too smart for that. He keeps us always
on our toes in the infield by reminding us how to play
certain hitters and what to be aware of in different situations. He would make a great manager. He knows all
about baseball strategy. Glenn sees things right away
that other players would miss. He keeps the whole
team alert and he never stops hustling. I've never seen
a player like him."

Glenn Beckert gets ready to make the double-play throw to first base as runner Dick Groat tries to obstruct the play.

In 1965, his rookie year, Glenn led the league's second basemen in assists and batted .239 in 154 games. He had 147 hits, and 120 of them were singles.

"I'll always be that way," he said. "I'm better off when I hit the ball on the ground. I'm dead when I hit it in the air. I don't want anyone to get the idea I'm against home runs, but trying for one hurts my batting. It's that way for a lot of fellows. The ones who just can't handle it will hurt themselves.

"If I hit a homer, it's always a surprise. I suppose you can say it's a big thrill, but when I hit 'em they mess me up. They can mess me up for two, maybe three weeks. When I get one, I think I can be a home run hitter again, and then I try to muscle all the pitches. It's a mistake. It's like Pete Reiser [a Cubs' coach] tells me. 'Beck,' he says, 'when you have two hundred and forty foot power, you don't try for the four hundred foot fences.' He's right."

In 1966 Glenn raised his average to a fine .287, and he collected 188 hits. His fielding still needed work—he led the league's second basemen in errors with 24. But he was one bright spot in a miserable year for the Cubs. In their first year under manager Leo Durocher they finished tenth of ten teams and lost 103 games. The next year the Cubs moved all the way up to third place and Beckert contributed a .280 batting average. He led the National League regulars for the second straight year in fewest strikeouts, and he teamed with shortstop Don Kessinger to give the Cubs the best-fielding pivot combination in the league.

In the tradition of Kenny Hubbs, Beckert was be-

Beckert dives for a ball off the bat of Joe Torre.

coming a superb fielder in his own right. In 1968 he
won the National League's Gold Glove, awarded by
the *Sporting News,* as the best fielding second baseman.
He committed only 19 errors in 817 total chances, for
a .977 fielding average, and he added several glowing
statistics as a batter. Glenn hit .294 that year, his best
average up to then. He had 189 hits, scored 98 runs to
lead the league, and struck out only 20 times in 643 at-
bats. He was named to two nationally-conducted All-
Star polls. It was a season to remember.

Then came 1969, a season to forget. The Cubs, who had led the league for much of the season, slumped badly in September and were hounded by the unlikely New York Mets, who until then had never finished higher than ninth place in their seven-year history.

Most of the reason for the Cubs' collapse, according to manager Leo Durocher, was a string of injuries to

A .343 hitter in 1971, Beckert begins his swing at the ball.

Beckert. Glenn collected 158 hits that season for a .291 average, second-best on the team, but he missed 31 games. Many times his presence in the line-up might have meant the difference between victory and defeat for Chicago.

The Cubs lost the pennant, and Beckert said it was the most disappointing period in his entire career. "I kept thinking it was my fault," he said, "and I just hated the thought of how close we had come. We were the team in first place. We should have held it. If we didn't start losing, the Mets never would have had a chance."

But in 1970 Glenn bounced back with another fine year. He missed only 19 games and batted .288. At mid-season he was elected by a national vote of fans as the starting second baseman on the National League All-Star team. And at the end of the season he was named to the *Sporting News* and Associated Press All-Star teams.

The year Beckert had been waiting for was 1971. Late in August he was fighting for the National League batting title with an average of .342. Then he suffered a broken thumb and was out the rest of the season. It was a sad way to end the year in which he improved both his hitting and his fielding. In 129 games he made only nine errors and compiled a fielding average of .986, the highest of his career.

Beckert was established as the National League's top second baseman. Durocher thought of him as "the heart of our team." He once said, "When Glenn hits, we score runs and we win. He is the winningest player I've ever seen or been associated with, right next to Willie Mays. He has a winning attitude and the talent to go with it. Every day he amazes me."

On a 1971 road trip to San Francisco the Cubs' bus was about to pull away from the stadium after a game.

Beckert, who was in the midst of a 27-game hitting streak, was late.

"Is everyone on?" Durocher asked.

"Everybody except Beckert," came the reply.

"Well, then stop this thing," Leo said. "He's the whole team right now. I wish I had twenty-five Glenn Beckerts around here. I wouldn't have to do a thing except sit back and relax."

Beckert had many accomplishments to look back on. He once got five hits in one game, and in September of 1970 he got his 1,000th hit in a game at Pittsburgh.

"But really," he said, "just being in the major leagues is enough of a thrill for me. Imagine, I was that skinny kid on the block, and today I'm in the majors. How could I expect to play in two All-Star games? Just being here is my true thrill, I suppose."

But Glenn looked ahead, too. "I want to play on a pennant team," he said. "And I want to play in the World Series. That would really be the top for me. I wouldn't want anything else after that."

Glenn Beckert became the major leaguer Kenny Hubbs might have been. If they had both been on the same Cubs' team, in the same infield, that Cub pennant might already have been won.

PEE WEE REESE
AND PHIL RIZZUTO

In the late 1930s two young men of about the same age were dreaming of baseball careers. Both of them were infielders and both showed tremendous talent. But there was one big problem. They were too short and too light. Harold Reese, who was called "Pee Wee," was 5-foot-9 and weighed less than 150 pounds. The other young man, Phil Rizzuto, was only 5-foot-6. But both of them fought their way to success, becoming the two leading shortstops of the 1940s and 1950s.

Pee Wee Reese signed a minor league contract with the Boston Red Sox after finishing high school. When a team offered a minor league contract, it meant that they did not expect the player to reach the majors. In those years the minor leagues were much more plentiful than they are now. The major league clubs all operated many "farm teams," and many players spent long careers as minor leaguers. The Red Sox thought Pee Wee would be one of these players.

Pee Wee signed the minor league contract because he thought he could prove the Red Sox wrong. But the Sox already had a superb shortstop named Joe Cronin, and they gave Pee Wee few chances to prove himself. So he asked the Red Sox to trade him or sell his contract to another team.

They agreed and sold him to the Brooklyn Dodgers' organization. But Reese had not solved his problem. The shortstop of the Dodgers was Leo Durocher, and he was the Dodger manager as well. Pee Wee still had little chance of breaking into the majors.

"I was upset," Pee Wee later recalled, "but I couldn't ask to be traded again. I had never played in the major leagues, and it just wouldn't have seemed right to keep asking to be traded until I found a team where I thought I had a chance. I decided to report to the Dodgers and just hope for the best."

In the spring of 1940 Pee Wee reported to the Dodgers' spring training camp in Vero Beach, Florida. He was frightened and unsure of himself. He had been sick for most of the winter and had lost weight. When he reported, he weighed barely 140 pounds and he was pale and nervous.

"Leo took one look at me," Pee Wee remembered, "and he said, 'Hey, kid, you look like you've been living in a closet. We'll have to fatten you up.' "

The Florida sunshine and the training routine were all that Reese needed. He gained ten pounds, began playing well and felt he had a good chance of making the team. He didn't know how good his chances were.

Leo Durocher had been thinking of retiring so that he could devote all his time to managing. He was just waiting until he found a younger man who could take over. He decided he had found that man in Pee Wee Reese.

"I made the team and we headed north," Pee Wee said later. "When the season started I played a few games, but not as a regular. Then toward the end of June, Leo just walked over to me and said, 'Kid, you're taking over my job tomorrow. Get ready.' "

Pee Wee couldn't sleep that night. "I would wake up every half hour and find myself shaking," he said. But the next day he did play, and he finished out the season as the regular Brooklyn shortstop. He did fairly well as a batter, hitting .272 with 28 runs-batted-in and 85 hits. In the field he proved that he was a shortstop of major league quality. He handled 428 chances and committed only 18 errors.

"I think I was nervous every game that season," he said. "I kept wondering how much the Dodgers liked me. I was afraid if I made an error, they'd take my job away and send me back to the minors."

Pee Wee remembers one game in that 1940 season vividly. One day his mother came to Cincinnati from her home in Kentucky to see him play. It was to be her first glimpse of her son as a major leaguer. "I made an error in the ninth inning, and because of it we lost the game," Pee Wee recalled. "I felt just awful." When all the other players had left the stadium, he was still in the locker room.

Red Corridan, a Dodger coach, came looking for Pee Wee. He found him just sitting there in the darkness.

"Your mother was here tonight, wasn't she?" Red asked.

Rookie Pee Wee Reese comes home after hitting a grand slam homer to beat the Giants in 1940.

"Yeah," Pee Wee murmured. "She must feel pretty lousy about the way I played. I'm embarrassed."

Corridan smiled. "I know how to make her feel better," he said. "When you walk out there to meet her now, just put on the biggest, brightest smile you've got. You're a major leaguer, and if you make an error, you're supposed to fight back. You can't let it get you down."

Pee Wee did as he was told, and Corridan followed him out. Sure enough, Pee Wee's mother was waiting, and his smile made her smile too. "That's when I knew he was going to be all right," Corridan said. "When he accepted defeat like a man."

Reese played regularly at shortstop in 1941 and 1942. Then he missed three seasons during World War II, serving in the armed forces like many other players. He returned to his regular position in 1946 and was a Dodger star for the next twelve years.

In 1949 Pee Wee led the league in runs scored and won the fielding championship for National League shortstops. It was the only time in his entire career that he won the fielding award. Jackie Robinson explained why: "He got to balls he had no business reaching. He had a fantastic range. I would see a ball hit on a line and it looked like it was going through the infield for sure. Then suddenly Pee Wee would have it. Sometimes he couldn't handle it all the way, but just getting to it was a miracle. Yet if he bobbled it, he drew an error. He was too good for his own good."

In 1941 the Dodgers had won their first pennant in 21 years. They won again in 1947. Beginning in 1949

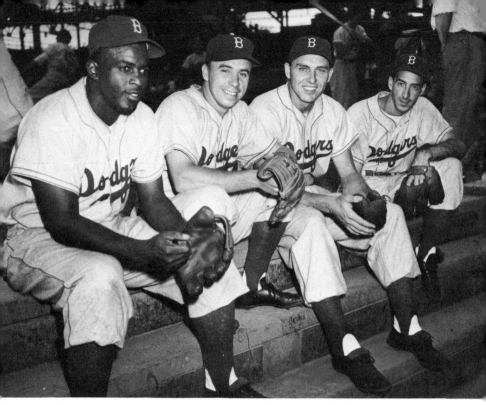

The great Dodger infield in 1949: Jackie Robinson, Reese, Gil Hodges and Billy Cox.

they dominated the National League, fielding one of the great teams in major-league history. Pee Wee shared the infield duties with Gil Hodges at first, Jackie Robinson at second and Billy Cox at third base. Reese and Robinson were a superb double-play combination.

Statistically, Pee Wee's greatest season was 1951 when he hit .286, drove in 84 runs and stole 20 bases. In 1954 he hit .309. Oddly enough, the Dodgers lost the pennant in both of these years to the New York Giants. They won it in 1952, 1953, 1955 and 1956. Reese played in seven World Series and batted over

.300 three times. In all, he got 46 World Series hits, ranking fifth in history.

Harold Henry Reese was born in Ekron, Kentucky, on July 23, 1918. His family soon moved to Louisville, where he attended grade school and where he acquired the nickname that would stick with him for the rest of his life.

"Sure, I was always small," he recalled, "but it wasn't for my size that I was called Pee Wee. I was a marbles shooter, and I got to be pretty good at it. Some of the marbles are called 'pee wees' and I just picked up the name. I got to the Kentucky State Pee Wee Marbles Championship when I was twelve years old, and after that all my friends started using the nickname."

By the time Pee Wee was a junior in high school, he weighed only 85 pounds and had decided to become a jockey. "Being from Louisville, which is a very horse-conscious area, it seemed natural to me," he remembered. "But I liked baseball, too, and when I got too heavy for horse-riding, I swung over to baseball. It's kind of funny. I was too big to be a jockey and almost too small to be a baseball player."

On the Dodgers Reese gained the job of keeping the team loose. His poise during crucial moments of important games helped relax his younger teammates. Junior Gilliam, who replaced Jackie Robinson at second base in 1953, later recalled Pee Wee's ability to help other players: "You just couldn't stay nervous with him on the team. I would go back for a pop-fly in a tough situation, and I'd start to get a little tense about it. Then I would hear him yelling, 'Don't get hit in the head, Jun-

In the 1952 World Series, the Yankees' Mickey Mantle upends Reese, trying to break up a double play.

ior!' Then I relaxed. Heck, I almost busted out laughing."

Pee Wee was also the Dodgers' practical joker. Once he tied Gil Hodges' favorite pair of slacks in knots when the team was on the field. When Hodges found the knotted slacks, he knew who was to blame and went to Reese's locker. There he found a sign: "Stay away from my slacks, Hodges."

During his later years with the Dodgers Pee Wee was faced with many challengers—bright young prospects wanted his job at shortstop. But each time, Pee Wee kept his job and the young players were traded to other teams by the satisfied Dodgers.

When Pee Wee neared the end of his career, the Dodgers asked him to accept the job as their manager. He turned it down. "I never thought I would like that kind of work," he said. "Hire someone else."

They did. His name was Walter Alston, and 18 seasons later he was still the Dodgers' manager, one of the most successful in baseball.

Phil Rizzuto grew up on the streets of Brooklyn in New York City. Like many city kids, he spent whole summers competing with his friends—often on a baseball field. But Phil had to be doubly good. As the smallest boy in the group, he had to make up in skill and fire what he lacked in size. When he played for the New York Yankees, Rizzuto stood 5-foot-6 and never weighed more than 150 pounds. The fact that he did play for the Yankees—for 16 seasons—is a tribute to his determination.

Philip Francis "Scooter" Rizzuto was born September 25, 1918, in the Ridgewood section of Brooklyn. He was small from the start. "I just never did start to grow normally," he said. "I was always the smallest kid in the neighborhood."

Phil's family had no time for sports. His father, an immigrant from Italy, worked as a conductor on a trolley car, then as a laborer for a construction company. Jobs were hard to find, and it was difficult to earn enough money to feed and clothe the family. But Phil's father was pleased that Phil had found an interest. "He always asked me about the baseball," Phil recalled. "I think he didn't want to admit he didn't understand it, but he was happy that I played. I know it bothered him when he heard the other kids laughing at me because of my size."

When the bigger boys chose sides for baseball, they picked Phil last. Then they sent him to the outfield where they felt he would do the least damage. They called him "shrimp" and "runt" and "half-pint." Phil didn't argue. But when the other boys saw him play, they soon began choosing him first instead of last.

Before Phil started high school, the Rizzutos moved to Richmond Hills, another section of New York City. At Richmond Hills High School Phil tried out as an outfielder for coach Al Kunitz. Kunitz saw right away that Rizzuto was too small to be an outfielder. He switched him to the infield and Phil had found a baseball home.

Kunitz told Phil that opponents would give him special attention because of his size. "Those base runners are going to slide in hard," he said. "They're going to stand up tall to try to block your vision. It won't be easy." But Kunitz encouraged Phil and tried to find him a tryout with one of the major league teams. In 1936 New York City had three teams—the Yankees, the New York Giants and the Brooklyn Dodgers. All the scouts came to watch Richmond Hills' games, but they weren't interested in Rizzuto.

On his own, Phil attended tryout camps run by all three teams. The Dodgers sent him home "to grow up a little." That judgement was made by Casey Stengel, who later managed the Yankees when Rizzuto was one of the main stars. The Giants weren't interested either. A scout named Pancho Snyder looked at Phil and said, "Go get a shoeshine box, kid, you'll never make the major leagues."

But a Yankee scout named Paul Kritchell saw some promise in Rizzuto. He invited Phil back to a series of tryout games, and finally he offered him a contract. Phil had his chance, and he began as an 18-year-old rookie on the Yankee farm team at Bassett, Virginia.

During that first season, he faced the biggest challenge of his life. Phil had pulled a muscle in his leg and had been playing in pain. At first he thought that there was nothing to worry about, but when the pain continued, Ray White, the manager of the Bassett team, persuaded him to see a doctor. The news was bad—a muscle had separated in his left thigh, and gangrene had set in. An operation was needed immediately. If the gangrene got worse or spread, it might force amputation of the leg.

"I thought my career was finished before it ever began," Phil said later. "I was the most scared eighteen year-old kid you ever saw. I was away from home for the first time in my life, and there wasn't time to think. It had to be done immediately. Really, I didn't have a choice, and I knew the doctor felt I would never be able to play baseball again."

The operation was successful, however, and the next year Phil was on his way again. He played for Bassett, Virginia; Norfolk, Virginia; and Kansas City, Missouri, then the Yankees' top farm team. On each team he showed great fielding ability and he was hitting well. He soon proved that he could compete with bigger men. Finally, in 1941, the Yankees added Phil Rizzuto to their major league roster.

The first day of spring training with the Yankees was one Phil never forgot. The guard at the entrance to the players' locker room wouldn't let him in. "He thought I was a kid looking for autographs," Phil said, "I had to get some of the Yankees to come out and vouch for me."

Rizzuto played 128 games at shortstop in 1941, taking the job away from veteran Frank Crosetti, who later became a Yankee coach. Phil batted .307 and drove in 46 runs. The Yanks won the pennant by 17 games, thanks to Phil and to a roster of all-time greats. The team included sluggers Joe DiMaggio, Charley Keller and Bill Dickey, second baseman Joe Gordon, and pitchers Lefty Gomez and Red Ruffing.

The Yanks won again in 1942. Phil hit .284 and

Phil Rizzuto poses in Yankee Stadium in 1950.

drove in 68 runs, and led the league's shortstops in put-outs and double plays. But World War II had begun, and Phil joined the Navy. He was out of baseball for the next three years, returning to the Yankees in 1946.

The Yankees won another pennant and World Series in 1947, then missed by a few games in 1948 to the Cleveland Indians. Then in 1949–53 they won five pennants and five World Series in a row—the first time in major league history that any team had dominated play so completely.

The years of 1949–53 were Rizzuto's most successful years, too. He started out the 1950 season the way all baseball players dream of starting. At the end of May he was batting over .400. His fielding was nearly flawless; he established a league record for most chances without an error—288. Phil's best plays were the two toughest for a shortstop to master: balls hit right up the middle over second base and those in the "deep area" between second and third. He turned many sure hits into outs, and more than a few of them became double plays.

As the season neared its end players and managers began suggesting that Rizzuto would be the league's Most Valuable Player. The manager of the St. Louis Browns, Zack Taylor, said after the Yanks had won a doubleheader, "I don't think the Yankees would have won without Phil on their side."

In the second game of that doubleheader Phil had demonstrated his game-winning talents. The Yanks led by one run in the ninth, but the Browns had loaded the bases with two out. Catcher Les Moss hit a low line drive up the middle, and the Yankees' one-run lead seemed doomed. But Phil chased the ball, then dived after it with his glove-hand outstretched. He stopped the ball, but it dropped to the ground. He picked it up and with his back to the infield, he flipped it to the second baseman for a force play to end the game.

When the season ended Phil had batted .324, gotten 200 hits and driven in 68 runs. He won the Golden

Rizzuto (left) fires the ball to first to complete a double play. Second baseman Gerry Coleman (right) started the play.

Glove award for shortstops, committing only 14 errors in 751 chances. As predicted, Rizzuto was named Most Valuable Player in the American League. The Yankees won the pennant, then took the World Series in four straight from Philadelphia.

In the 1951 World Series the Yankees beat the Giants in six games. But in the third game Phil was victimized by another fierce competitor, the Giants' Eddie Stanky, in the famous "kick ball" incident. The Giants held a 1-0 lead in the fifth inning. Stanky, the Giants' second baseman, began the inning with a walk.

Then he broke for second on the first pitch to the next batter, attempting a steal.

The Yankee catcher, Yogi Berra, had expected the steal and called for a pitchout. Rizzuto was covering the base, and Berra's throw was perfect. But when Eddie slid in, he swung his foot up and kicked the ball out of Phil's hand. Phil was too surprised to move immediately, and the clever Stanky got up and raced to third safely. Stanky's play began a five-run inning for the Giants and they won the game 6-2.

Rizzuto never forgave Stanky for causing him such embarrassment, and the two men continued their feud for the next twenty years. "Rizzuto should have tagged him right in the teeth with that ball," said Casey Stengel, the Yankee manager. "It was a good play by Stanky, and a lousy one by Phil. He should know better."

It was the only bad moment of an otherwise splendid World Series for the Scooter. Phil batted .320 and even hit a home run, which was a rare accomplishment for him. He drove in three runs and scored five.

In 1954 the Yankees' string of pennants was finally snapped by the Cleveland Indians, who set a league record of 111 victories. It was Phil's final season as a regular, and his batting average slipped all the way down to .195. He knew he was near the end of his career, but he turned down offers from other teams to become a playing manager. "I'll stay with the Yankees until they don't want me," he said loyally. "They're my team. My only team."

Two years later, in the early part of the 1956 season,

the Yankees gave Phil his unconditional release. General manager George Weiss broke the sad news to Rizzuto. Phil was stunned. Then tears came to his eyes. He groped his way to the team locker room, where he packed his belongings and went home.

A year later Rizzuto became one of the Yankee announcers on radio and television. He was one of the first former players to become an announcer and his fans appreciated his first-hand experience. Fifteen years later he was still a popular Yankee broadcaster.

"If I can give the fans tips on the game, reasons why certain plays worked and others didn't, I feel I am doing something more than the next announcer," he said. "It was frightening at first. I wasn't sure of what to say or how to say it. But I learned." Looking back on his two successful careers, in baseball and in broadcasting, he summed up the secret of his success. "It's all in how much you want to do it," he said.

In the famous "kick ball" incident, Rizzuto gets set to tag Stanky (top), puts the tag on him (center), and has the ball kicked out of his glove (bottom). Stanky went to third.

LUIS APARICIO

In 1970 Luis Aparicio changed his Sox—from Chicago White to Boston Red. It was the third time he had been traded in his long career, and he had a chance to gain a following of fans in Boston like those he had left in Chicago and Baltimore.

After 16 major league seasons, little Luis had fans everywhere. He had set a number of American League fielding and stolen bases records, and had played on eight American League All-Star teams and two World Series teams. He was a confident, self-assured veteran.

Luis Aparicio had come a long way since he first arrived in the United States as a boy of 19. He had come from Maracaibo, Venezuela, to play with a Chicago White Sox minor league team. He spoke no English. He brought no clothes. "I didn't know how to dress or what to eat or where to go," he remembered. "I was very much a lost boy."

Luis was new to America, but he was not new to baseball. The game is as popular in Central and South America and the Caribbean as it is in the United States. Luis had played the game from the time he could hold a bat. His father was Venezuela's best known baseball star—a national hero. By the time his father was ready to retire after 18 years with the Gavilanes team, Luis was ready to take his place. Gavilanes' fans saw the son play the same position as the father and soon Luis was becoming the same sort of hero.

"My father did everything for me in baseball," Luis later recalled. "From the time I was a little boy he played with me. He brought home baseballs and bats and gloves. I was throwing and catching as soon as I could walk. I loved baseball, and I dreamed of the day I would be able to play well enough to make my father happy. When it came to baseball, he was not an easy man to please."

But playing with the Venezuelan team, Luis soon attracted the attention of major league scouts with his flashy fielding and solid hitting. American baseball was just beginning to discover how talented and well-trained the Latin American players were.

Two teams, the White Sox and the Cleveland Indians, made attractive offers to Luis. A chance remark by

Hank Greenberg, who was then Cleveland's vice president, turned Luis to Chicago. "Greenberg said I was too small to be a good big league player," Luis said. "He said it to some people, and I heard about it. It bothered me. So I signed the White Sox contract. I think I would have signed with Cleveland until then, you know."

So 19-year-old Luis Aparicio set out on a journey to a strange country to play among strangers. It was a big adventure, for he had doubts and fears and a language barrier to overcome.

Chicago's minor league director, Glen Miller, met Luis' airplane at Miami's International Airport in the winter of 1954. He was surprised by what he saw.

"I was looking for a baseball player as the people started filing out of the plane," he said, "and then I saw this handsome, dark-haired boy who didn't seem more than fifteen years old walking towards me. He couldn't speak a word of English but he kept saying 'Aparicio, Aparicio' so I knew it was him. He was a lot smaller than I had expected him to be, but when he took part in his first workout the next day, I saw the style and the talent our scouts had seen."

Luis was not yet ready for the majors. He spent his first year in America in Waterloo, Iowa. He adjusted quickly to his new surroundings. He batted .282, and drove in 47 runs while scoring 85. It was not all easy, however. Many times Luis got discouraged. A fear of failure kept him from turning back. "I didn't think I could go back home and say I didn't want to play in America," Luis stated. "My father's reputation as a

White Sox rookie Luis Aparicio in 1956.

player, and mine, were too important. I couldn't fail."

The next year the White Sox moved Luis up to Memphis, Tennessee, in the Southern Association. He led the league with 48 stolen bases, hit .273, scored 92 runs and drove in 51. He led the league in put-outs and assists, but tied for the lead in errors. Like other great shortstops, Luis covered so much ground that he had to make errors. He made errors on some balls that other shortstops could not have reached. Luis was on the way to the White Sox.

"I thought I was ready," he recalled later. "After that season in Memphis, I felt I could play major league baseball."

But in 1956 when he reported to the team's spring training camp in Sarasota, Florida, all the veteran players saw was a 5-foot-8, 155-pound rookie. The White Sox had finished third in 1955 and felt sure they had a team strong enough to win the pennant the next season. They needed a major-league shortstop, but they couldn't believe that little Luis, frail and slight, could be the answer.

But when the team began its exhibition games, Luis became the sensation of the camp. The White Sox were so enthusiastic about him that they traded the regular shortstop of the year before, Chico Carrasquel, to Cleveland.

Aparicio was the fanciest fielding shortstop the White Sox had ever seen and one of the flashiest base runners in memory. Nellie Fox, one of the game's finest second basemen and Luis' teammate for many years with the White Sox, couldn't believe that a player so young had as much training and polish.

"He was a trained fielder even then," Fox said. "He needed only experience and the knowledge of where to play the different hitters. Luis picked up these points quickly, because he was a sharp fellow who had a serious approach to the game. He hounded a ball real good, and his best asset was his quick hands. He charged a ball better than anyone I ever saw, and he went into the hole for those deep line drives and ground smashes very well."

As a rookie, Aparicio led the league's shortstops in put-outs, assists—and errors. As in the minor leagues, he got to more balls and sometimes received an error for a mistake on a spectacular play. He batted .266 and led the league with 21 stolen bases. He was voted Rookie of the Year by a large margin.

Al Lopez became the new White Sox manager in 1957, and the first statement he made was about the White Sox's infield. "With Aparicio and Fox, we have the finest double play combination in the league," he said. "Luis makes every play in the book. . . . I don't remember seeing a better fielding shortstop, nor anyone quite as dangerous on the basepaths, either."

Indeed, Aparicio's baserunning became his trademark, and the team's as well. They became known as the "Go Go White Sox" and Luis was the "goingest" of them all. When Luis reached first base, the fans in Chicago's Comiskey Park would automatically begin to chant, "Go! Go! Go!" Very often Luis went. He studied the pitchers and knew which ones he could take advantage of. He timed his breakneck rush toward

Aparicio slides home safely in a 1956 game.

second perfectly with the pitcher's delivery, giving the
catcher little time to throw him out.

Whitey Ford was perhaps the finest left-handed
pitcher in the league in those years. Even though left-
handers are difficult to steal on since they face first base
during their windup, Ford recalled "feeling chills"
whenever Aparicio got on. "You just couldn't keep
him near the base," Ford said. "He was the most
aggravating little so-and-so I ever had to worry about."

Luis developed his base-stealing skills quickly, leading the league in each of his first three seasons with 21, 28 and 29. But his fourth year, 1959, was the big one for him and for the White Sox.

For four years in a row the Yankees had won the American League pennant. They were the most feared team in the league, boasting great hitters, such as Mickey Mantle, Yogi Berra, Hank Bauer and Moose Skowron, and a fine pitching staff. In the past ten years they had won the pennant nine times, and in 1959 they were favored to win it again.

The White Sox had pitching and defense, fielding and speed. But they had no power hitting. In 1958 the whole team had hit only 101 homers, the fewest in the league. Only one hitter had hit .300 (Nellie Fox hit .300 exactly but hadn't hit a single home run). The outlook for 1959 was not hopeful if the Sox were compared to the powerful Yankees.

But the White Sox won that 1959 pennant anyway. They pecked and nibbled away at pitchers. They used singles, stolen bases and sacrifices to score runs. Even then they scored only 668 runs for the season, compared to Cleveland's league-leading total of 745. But their outstanding pitching staff, which included Early Wynn (22 10), Bob Shaw (18-6), Billy Pierce (14-15) and Turk Lown (9-2), allowed opposing teams only 588 runs. They didn't score many runs, but they gave up even less.

The White Sox also frustrated their opponents with their flawless fielding. Fox and Aparicio each led the league in fielding at their positions. Luis led the league's shortstops in put-outs, assists and fielding average, and won the Golden Glove award.

Luis also stunned the baseball world with his base stealing. His total for the year was 56. Only two men had stolen more bases in a season since 1920. The second-place finisher in 1959 was Mickey Mantle with 21. In one game, against the Boston Red Sox, Aparicio stole four bases. Twice he stole second, once he stole third and once he stole home, and the White Sox won the game 2-1.

Luis was no power hitter, but he enjoyed a good season at bat. He batted .257 and drove in 51 runs. In addition he drew 52 walks. In his 664 times up, he reached base 215 times. Then he improved his position by stealing a base 56 times. He proved that a player can help his team to a pennant without hitting over .300 or blasting home runs.

The White Sox won the pennant easily, finishing five games ahead of Cleveland and 15 games ahead of the Yankees. In the World Series they faced the Los Angeles Dodgers, another team with a no-power, all-speed offense, and a great pitching staff. The Dodgers won the Series, four games to two. But Luis had a good performance record, batting .308 and stealing two bases.

The White Sox fell from the top to third place in 1960 and 1961. Aparicio increased his value to the team with his continued excellence in fielding and baserunning. He had the highest fielding average among shortstops in both years, stole over 50 bases and brought his batting average up above .270.

In 1962 neither Luis nor the White Sox had much to be happy about. The Sox finished fifth and Luis' batting average fell to .241. Still, he led the league once again in stolen bases and in fielding average for shortstops. Along with the Cubs' Ernie Banks, he was Mr. Baseball in Chicago.

Then the White Sox made a surprise move. Seeking to strengthen their team at other infield positions and at the plate, they announced a major trade on January 14,

Playing for Baltimore, Aparicio does a little dance to avoid being picked off first base by the Red Sox' Dick Stuart.

1963. Aparicio was sent to the Baltimore Orioles, along with outfielder Al Smith, in exchange for four Baltimore players.

"I was really upset," Luis recalled later. "The trade was something that hurt me. I had played seven years with the White Sox. Chicago was my second home. I loved the people and the city and the team. Then I was traded, and I decided I would do all I could to make the Orioles happy. They wanted me badly enough to make such a deal, and I wanted to make them proud."

Luis picked up in Baltimore where he had left off in Chicago. Baltimore was a young team just beginning to climb in the league standings. Aparicio steadied the young players, batted .250, and led the league's short-stops with a .983 fielding average. He led the American League in stolen bases with 40, but Maury Wills, another shortstop, stole 104 bases in the National League, setting an all-time record.

Soon Luis became as popular in Baltimore as he had been in Chicago. The Orioles' fans began the familiar "Go! Go! Go!" chant when he reached base. Slowly the Orioles improved. In 1965 they added Boog Powell at first base, and in 1966 Dave Johnson became the regular second baseman. Teaming with Aparicio and third baseman Brooks Robinson, they made up a prize-winning infield. In the outfield the Orioles gained the services of Frank Robinson and Paul Blair. For the first time the Orioles were on the pennant trail, finishing the 1966 season nine games in front.

Aparicio made a big contribution. He stole 25 bases, batted .276 and scored 97 runs. He led the league's shortstops in fielding average for the eighth consecutive year, a major-league record. In the World Series—against the Dodgers—the Orioles were heavy favorites, but no one expected them to sweep the Dodgers in four games. They beat Don Drysdale twice, Sandy Koufax once and Claude Osteen once, to embarrass the National League champions. Luis had four hits and drove in a pair of runs. In the final two games, each of which Baltimore won by a 1-0 score, he was brilliant in the field, making four key plays with men on base.

Baltimore fell all the way to sixth place in 1967, losing more games than they won. After the season Luis found himself traded again, this time back to the White Sox. He had not had a good season and Baltimore wanted younger men. They got infield-outfield star Don Buford and two pitchers for Aparicio.

"If I had to be traded, I was happy it was Chicago that wanted me," Luis said. Luis played well with the White Sox in 1968, and in 1969 he had one of his best seasons. He played in 156 games and batted .280, the highest average of his career. In 1970 he even improved that record, batting .313 in 157 games. He ranked fourth in the league. His fielding average was still near the top of the league, although at 36 he had slowed down a step or two.

Then Luis had another shock. In December of 1970 the White Sox announced that they had traded Luis again, this time to the Boston Red Sox. If he was discouraged, Aparicio didn't show it. The Red Sox moved their great shortstop Rico Petrocelli to second to make

Aparicio completes a double play in 1971 for his new team, the Boston Red Sox.

room for Aparicio, and Luis played regularly.

"When I came to this country, I can't speak English," he said in a recent interview. "I don't know anybody. I am very nervous and worried. But everyone was good to me. They go out of their way to help me. I owe baseball so much that I can never pay back. I am the luckiest man I know. I came to a strange country and I have made money, friends and memories that I will keep for all time."

KEN AND CLETE BOYER

When Ken Boyer was growing up in Liberty, Missouri, all he wanted was to be as good a baseball player as his older brother Cloyd. When Clete Boyer was growing up in Cassville, Missouri, a few years later he wanted to be as good a baseball player as his older brother Ken. All three brothers made it to the big leagues, and both Ken and Clete became star third basemen.

There have been many brother acts in major league baseball: Dizzy and Paul Dean; Joe, Vince and Dom DiMaggio; Jim and Gaylord Perry; the three Alou brothers, Matty, Felipe and Jesus; and others.

Clete Boyer (left) and his brother Ken pose before their teams meet in the 1964 World Series.

But the Boyers were special. Both became All-Stars, both were third basemen and at one time they were regarded as the finest third basemen in their leagues. The two Boyers both arrived in the majors in the same year and they even faced each other in the 1964 World Series.

Although Ken and Clete had different strengths, it was difficult to say which was better. Ken was a feared slugger who finished his 14-year career with a .288 batting average, 282 home runs and 1,137 RBI's. He was named Most Valuable Player in the National League in 1964. Clete hit only .240 with 126 homers and 516 RBI's. But Clete was a spectacular fielder, one of the best ever seen in the majors.

Ken was a strong hitter who could field, and Clete was a great fielder who could hit. Between them, they became the most famous brother combination in recent years, as well as two of the finest third basemen in baseball.

Kenton Lloyd Boyer was born on May 20, 1931, in Liberty, Missouri. He grew to 6-foot-2 and 190 pounds, and he was big even as a boy. "I remember being one of the biggest kids around," he said, "and so I was the guy everybody expected to do well in sports. I played all of them—football, baseball and basketball —but I quickly decided baseball was my favorite. I guess it was an easy choice, because by the time I was able to play, my older brother, Cloyd, was already a star."

In fact Cloyd was the first of the three Boyers to make it to the major leagues. Ken was 18 years old and beginning his first season in the minor leagues when Cloyd was a rookie pitcher with the Cardinals. Ken had signed with the Cards as a pitcher, too, hoping to follow his brother to St. Louis. Unfortunately, Cloyd didn't stay long with the Cards. And before Ken arrived in the big leagues he had been shifted from pitcher to third base. He was too good a hitter for the managers to use him just once every four or five days.

"If anything made me happy, that was it," he remembered later. "Ever since I was very young, I wanted to play all the time. But I happened to be a better pitcher than anything else when I was a boy, and if that was going to take me to the major leagues, I was content to pitch. But in the back of my mind, I always wished I could play all the time. I loved to hit, not just pitch, and I loved to play."

When Ken was growing up, times were hard for the Boyer family. There were twelve children and money was scarce. "I remember selling magazines, working on farms in the area and plowing or harvesting for a day's pay even when I was young," he said. "I gave half my money to my parents. But there was time for fun."

For fun, Boyer and his brothers could hitchhike nine miles to Webb City for a movie or swim in the pit of an abandoned mine shaft. Their father helped them clear a makeshift baseball field across from their home, and there was time to play ball.

"Mostly, it was sports, and by the time I reached high school, I knew I wanted to be a professional baseball player. It was all I thought about," Ken recalled.

After high school Ken signed a $6,000 contract with the Cardinals. He gave half the money to his parents. He started out on a Cardinal farm team, but before he had advanced very far, the Korean War broke out. Ken spent the 1952 and 1953 seasons in the armed forces. When he returned, the Cards sent him to Houston, their top minor league team. He had a fine season, finishing with a .319 batting average, 21 homers and 116 RBI's.

The next year, 1955, the Cards called him to the

major leagues. They were so confident of their star rookie that they traded away their regular third baseman, Ray Jablonski, to the Cincinnati Reds. As a result, Ken was actually a Cardinal regular before he played his first game.

As a rookie he hit .264, drove in 62 runs, slammed 18 homers, and proved his major league fielding ability. Despite his great performance, he lost the Rookie of the Year award to another Cardinal rookie, Bill Virdon, an outfielder who had hit .281.

Still, Ken had established himself as a regular with great potential, and he received a healthy raise for the 1956 season. He earned his money, achieving the first of many .300 seasons. He hit .306 and added 26 homers and 65 RBI's. In the field he played in 149 games and had more assists and more double plays than any other third baseman in the league.

Ken was not a colorful player and he had his troubles with St. Louis fans. Even when he was playing well and leading the league in several departments they often booed him on the field.

"I never understood it, but it never bothered me much," Ken said. "If they wanted to boo, well, it was their right. They paid for the ticket. I just tried to do my best."

His other trouble at St. Louis was with Frank Lane, the St. Louis general manager. Lane was a famous baseball trader. When he decided that Ken wasn't enough of a hustler, he arranged a deal with Pittsburgh. The Pirates would receive Boyer in exchange for a powerful outfielder and an infielder. But when

August Busch, the owner of the Cardinals, heard about it, he refused to permit the trade. After the 1957 season Frank Lane quit.

The new general manager, Bing Devine, later received a tempting offer for Boyer. The Cardinals were still seeking a power-hitting outfielder and the Philadelphia Phillies offered centerfielder Richie Ashburn *and* pitcher Harvey Haddix for Boyer. But Devine felt something was wrong.

"It's a fair deal, considering all things," he told a newspaperman, "but I'll stake my reputation on Ken Boyer. I think he'll become a great player, and if he realizes his potential, he can take Stan Musial's place as the highest-paid Cardinal."

So Devine called off the trade. Instead, he made a deal with Cincinnati, obtaining a young outfielder named Curt Flood, who became a big star for the Cards.

Ken stayed with St. Louis. From 1958 through 1963 he hit over .300 four times. In 1961 he hit .329 with 95 RBI's and 24 homers. He became, as Devine predicted, a great Cardinal player, an All-Star and the highest-paid man on the St. Louis roster.

But something was missing—a pennant. The fans of St. Louis were eager to see their team in a World Series. The Cards were good: they came in third in 1960 and second in 1963, but each year they fell short of the pennant. During the spring training period of 1964, however, the whole team was optimistic. They felt this would be their year.

Ken spoke to an interviewer that spring and predicted a pennant for the Cardinals. "We have the best team in the National League," he said. "We had the best team last year, but we made our own mistakes. This time we'll win. I am unhappy with my career because I haven't played on a championship team yet. If I am as good as people say, I should have been able to help my team win a pennant."

The Cardinals proved that they were the best team in 1964. Bill White, the first baseman, hit .303 with 102 RBI's. He also won the National League's Golden Glove Award as the best-fielding first baseman. Shortstop Dick Groat hit .292 and teamed with Julian Javier at second and Boyer at third to make a superb infield. Tim McCarver, a .288 hitter, was the catcher, and the outfield was made up of Lou Brock (.348), Curt Flood (.311) and Mike Shannon (.261).

Boyer had a banner year. Although his average dropped to .295, he drove in a league-leading total of 119 runs and slammed out 24 homers. Ken was best in clutch situations, and he supplied the steadiness the Cards needed in the last weeks of the close pennant race. Time and again he saved games with a clutch play at third or a timely hit.

"He always made the big plays," said Bob Gibson, the Cardinals' fast-balling right-hander. "Whenever we were in a tight spot, Ken came up with what we needed. I think he personally won ten of my nineteen games for me with either a run batted in or a big fielding play."

The Cardinals battled with the Reds and Phillies right down to the final day of the season. They finished

Ken Boyer takes a hopelessly high throw from the catcher as the Mets' Chico Fernandez steals third.

with a 93-69 record while the Reds and Phillies finished in a tie for second, just one game behind at 92-70. The Cardinals had won the chance to play in the World Series, and Ken Boyer was chosen Most Valuable Player in the National League.

The Cards faced the New York Yankees in the Series, and Ken played opposite his brother Clete, the Yanks' third baseman. The Yankees built a two to one edge in the first three games. If they won the fourth game, it would be almost impossible for the Cards to

save themselves. The Yankees took a 3-0 lead in the first inning. New York's pitcher, Al Downing, who made a dramatic comeback with the Los Angeles Dodgers in 1971, pitched shutout ball through five innings.

Then in the sixth the Cards started a rally. With one out Carl Warwick pinch-hit a single, and Curt Flood followed with another. Then Groat hit a grounder to the Yanks' Bobby Richardson at second base. It seemed to be a sure double-play ball. Bobby had been the fielding hero of the 1962 World Series, making a spectacular catch of Willie McCovey's line drive to end the seventh game. But he bobbled this simple grounder, and the Cards had the bases loaded.

The next man up was Ken Boyer.

"I remember thinking to myself when Groat hit that ball that Richardson owed me something," Boyer recalled later. "But I was the most surprised man in the stadium when he let the ball get past him. Then, all of a sudden, I realized I was up next and the bases were loaded. We were losing by three runs. I never even thought about hitting a home run. It would have been too corny."

Ken Boyer did hit a home run, though, and the Cards won the game 4-3. They went on to win the Series in seven games. In the final game Ken hit another homer, driving in the winning run.

Ken played just one more season with the Cards. He was traded to the New York Mets for the 1966 season. He was traded to the Chicago White Sox in mid-1967 and then to the Los Angeles Dodgers in 1968. After his retirement he joined the Cardinals as a coach.

Fred Hutchinson, who was manager of the Cards from 1956 through 1958, summed up Ken's value to the team: "Ken is the kind of player you wish you had twelve of. You could have nine on the field and three on the bench. He's the kind of guy you dream about—terrific speed, great arm and brute strength."

In 1961 Fred Hutchinson was the manager of the Cincinnati Reds. When the Reds played the Yankees in the World Series, he had a close-up view of Clete Boyer. Although he would not compare the two brothers, he was amazed at Clete's performance.

Ken Boyer hits the home run that beat the Yankees in the fourth game of the 1964 World Series.

"I have seen," he said. "Clete is something special."

Cletis LeRoy Boyer was born February 8, 1937, in Cassville, Missouri. He was six years younger than Ken, but he broke into the major leagues the same year as his brother. Clete was only 18 and Ken was nearly 24.

Clete signed with the Kansas City Athletics (who later moved to Oakland). He was a "bonus baby" in 1955, and under an old major league rule, the Athletics were required to keep him on their major league roster for two years. If it had not been for this "bonus baby" rule, Clete might have been the third Boyer brother to sign with St. Louis. The Cards already had one bonus baby on their bench, and they were preparing to add another, pitcher Lindy McDaniel. Since the inexperienced bonus players seldom contributed much to the team, the Cardinals felt they could not afford to sign a third one.

Clete signed a $35,000 contract with Kansas City, then spent most of his time on the bench for three years. The A's had not even decided what position he should play. Manager Lou Boudreau tried him at second, third, short and the outfield.

Then after the 1957 season Kansas City made an 11-player trade with the Yankees. Boyer and four others went to New York. The Yankees were sure they had a prospect in Clete, but they felt he still needed experience. So after three years in the majors Clete found himself in Richmond of the International League. He stayed there for 1958 and part of 1959 before being brought up to the Yankees.

Boyer's "second" major league career began in 1960. He played in 124 games for the Yanks at third and shortstop. The Yankees won the first of what were to be five straight pennants, and Clete began to show the league what a fielder he was.

Fred Hutchinson saw Clete in the 1961 World Series against Cincinnati. During this Series many fans first noticed Clete's play at third base. He was nicknamed "The Vacuum Cleaner" for the way he scooped up everything hit anywhere near third base,

Clete Boyer shows how he became known as the "Vacuum Cleaner" as he grabs a hard smash by Frank Robinson in the 1961 Series.

and his plays helped the Yankees sweep the Series in four straight games.

Frank Crosetti, who was a Yankee player and coach from 1932 through 1969, became Boyer's number one fan. "I got to the Yankees too late to see Joe Dugan [another fancy-fielding third baseman]," Crosetti said. "But I have seen everybody since, and this man is the best. What can't he do?"

Boyer's style was heart-stopping. He played closer to the batter than almost any third baseman ever had, as though he were daring the hitters to hit the ball past him. And they couldn't. When they did connect with screaming line drives or hard-hit smashes on the ground, Clete would dive, come up with the ball and throw them out while still on the ground.

"He was able to do that because he had tremendous arm power," Crosetti said. "He not only threw hard when he was down, but he threw strikes. I've never seen a man field that way. His glove seemed to be a separate living thing. There were times when I would have bet anything that the ball was going to be at least a double, and I was wondering if even the outfielders could get to it. Then he'd have it in his glove. I swear he used magic."

Clete was never a top hitter. His highest average for a season was .272, and he hit 18 home runs in two different years. In the 1962 Series he did bat .318 and won the first game with a home run in the seventh inning. But the Yankees were usually content to let other players pick up for Clete at the plate—no one else had his magic glove.

After winning five straight pennants, the Yankees fell on hard times. They finished sixth in 1965 and tenth in 1966, the first time they finished last in nearly 50 years. Changes had to be made. Clete was traded to the Atlanta Braves for an outfielder named Bill Robinson, who was supposed to become the next great Yankee hitter.

Robinson was a disappointment and never contributed much to the Yankees. But Clete turned in some of his best years for the Braves. In 1967 he hit a career-high of 26 home runs and drove in 96 runs. He also won the National League's Golden Glove Award as the third baseman with the highest fielding average—.970. Clete had never won a Golden Glove Award when he was with the Yankees, despite his reputation as the fanciest of fielders.

The Braves won the National League's Western Division championship in 1969, but lost to the New York Mets in the league playoff series. It was Clete's last glimpse of championship games. In 1970, while batting .246 with 16 homers and 62 runs batted in, Clete began a long argument with Atlanta's general manager, Paul Richards. In 1971 he finally demanded his release and he finished out the year playing for Honolulu of the Pacific Coast League.

During his 15 years in the major leagues, Clete developed a daring style of play at third base that many young players tried to copy. He had the fastest glove in the East, and he often made the plays that won games.

"I always felt a third baseman should play up close, and be able to make the plays on line drives anyway,"

Clete falls into the stands trying to get a foul ball.

he once said. "I enjoy fielding from up close like that. You know, the ball comes at you so fast you don't have the time to think about it, and when you begin to play instinctively, you're better. Besides, you're so much closer to those slow rollers down the line."

Three of the Boyer brothers had already played in the majors, and it seemed possible that more would follow. A fourth brother, Len, was playing in the St. Louis farm system, and a fifth, Ron, was in the Yankees' system.

But Ken and Clete were enough to make the Boyer name unforgettable. When fans talked about great third basemen, these two brothers were always high on the list—one of the greatest brother acts in baseball.

BROOKS ROBINSON

It is the first game of the 1970 World Series. Cincinnati is at bat in the sixth against Baltimore and the score is tied 3-3. First baseman Lee May, one of the Reds' most feared sluggers, is at bat.

The pitcher throws a hanging curve, an easy pitch to hit. May times the swing of his bat perfectly. Smack! He hits a vicious line drive, sinking fast, down the third base line. It seems like a sure double. The Cincinnati fans jump to their feet cheering.

Suddenly the roar stops. Brooks Robinson, the Oriole third baseman, backhands the ball, pivots in foul territory and fires a strike to first base. May is out. In the next inning Robinson hits a home run and the Orioles win 4-3.

It is the second game of the 1970 World Series. The Reds are leading 4-0. Their men are on first and second base when May comes up again. He drives another wicked liner down toward third. Again Robinson snares the ball back-handed and starts a third-to-second-to-first double play to end the inning. Two innings later Robinson singles in the go-ahead run and scores another, and the Orioles take the second game 6-5.

"Nobody could have fielded those balls," said a startled May. "Nobody except Brooks Robinson would have had a chance."

Brooks Robinson makes a near-impossible stop of Johnny Bench's drive in the 1970 World Series. He threw Bench out.

The Orioles went on to win the 1970 World Series in five easy games. Brooks made two other near-impossible plays. He had nine hits, including two homers and two doubles, a .429 batting average and six RBI's. He was voted the Series' Most Valuable Player. The baseball world already had agreed that Robinson was the greatest all-round third baseman of recent times.

"He was incredible," said the Reds' Pete Rose, a two-time National League batting king with a .309 lifetime average. "I think he could have played third base with a pair of pliers."

A year earlier the Orioles and Robinson were in a different mood. They were champions of the American League, playing in the World Series against the unlikely New York Mets, surprise winners of the National League pennant.

The Orioles were heavy favorites. People said the Series would go no more than five games. They were right, but it was the Mets who won in one of baseball's great upsets. Baltimore was humiliated and so was Brooks Robinson.

"We were too relaxed," he said later. "We believed all those things people wrote in the newspapers, about how easy it would be for us to beat the Mets. We didn't think they had a chance, and we played that way. I was terrible. I just kept waiting for them to make their mistakes. I waited and I waited, and suddenly they were the world champions. I'll never forget how badly I felt."

After 1970 Brooks was more philosophical about the loss to the Mets. "It brought us together as a team," he said. "Losing to the Mets helped us grow up. I'm not glad we lost, but it was the best thing that could have happened to us. It made us the great team we are."

Brooks Calbert Robinson, Jr., was born May 18, 1937, in Little Rock, Arkansas. In junior high school he played in all three major sports, delivered newspapers, worked at odd jobs and maintained a B-average in school.

"I liked all the sports, but baseball was something special," he said years later. "In junior high I was the quarterback for Pulaski Heights and I played well. But I chose not to play football in high school, because I wanted to be a major league baseball player and a guy could get hurt playing football. Everything I did as a boy centered around baseball."

Brooks played second and third base in high school and played well enough to attract 15 major league teams. In his senior year he had a big decision to make. He had been offered a four-year baseball scholarship to the University of Arkansas. His mother and father thought he should take it. "You can play baseball there," said his dad, "and then sign with the major leagues when you graduate."

But Brooks felt differently. He worried that he would be thinking too much about baseball to concentrate on his studies. He wanted a chance to play right away.

His parents finally agreed, and on May 29, 1955, the day after Brooks graduated from Little Rock High, he and his dad listened to offers from nine major league scouts. Then they narrowed the choice down to Baltimore or Cincinnati. Art Ehlers, the Orioles' assistant general manager, finally got Brooks' signature.

"We think you can make the major leagues," he had told Brooks, "but not yet. Your speed isn't very good and your arm is only fair. But you can field and hit. We would want to farm you down, but we are a

Rookie Brooks Robinson during 1957 spring training.

young team and we'll need all the young players we can get. Your chances with us are excellent. All we can offer is a $4,000 contract, but it's a chance to get to Baltimore quickly."

The next day Brooks made up his mind. He called the Reds' scout and turned down their larger offer. "I'm going with the Orioles," he said. "I'll have a chance to get to the major league team faster."

Brooks flew to Baltimore with Ehlers the next day, and after he had spent a few days with the Orioles, he was sent to the York team in the Piedmont League. He played in 95 games that summer and hit .331 with 67 runs-batted-in. He played second and third, fielded well and pleased the Orioles.

When the York season ended, Brooks was brought up to the Orioles, and in the first game he played in the majors, against the Washington Senators, he got two hits and drove in the winning run.

When the game was over, he rushed to a telephone to call his parents in Little Rock. "I don't know why I've been playing in the minors," said the 18-year-old Robinson. "I should have been here all along."

In his next 18 times at bat, Brooks struck out ten times and did not get another hit. "I learned that you have to work hard to get anywhere," he said, smiling, "and I learned not to make any more phone calls."

Brooks spent the next four seasons partly with the Orioles and partly in the minor leagues. He played at San Antonio and Vancouver, and in 1958 he played 145 games for the Orioles and led the league's third basemen in put-outs. But he batted a disappointing

Robinson makes a great recovery after knocking down a grounder by Bobby Richardson and throws him out at first.

.238. In 1959 he started the season back in the minors, but then he returned to Baltimore and hit .284 in 88 games.

Brooks remembered his early days as a major leaguer, and the trouble he had hitting curves. "I just couldn't get the timing down right," he said once. "The big, tall pitchers with the sweeping curves used to drive me crazy. I am sure this was the reason why I kept getting sent down to the minors. But a man named Joe Schultz helped me. He explained that you shouldn't try to hit that curve where it seems to be, but time it so that you can hit where it will be when it crosses the plate. It's called going with the pitch. If I have anything to offer young players trying to improve their hitting, it's that. Patience is the thing that makes you a good hitter. The way pitchers are today, with such good stuff, they can really make you look bad if you're too anxious."

In 1960, his first full major league season, Brooks hit .294, slammed 14 homers and drove in 88 runs. He also led the league's third basemen in fielding. In the next eleven years he led the league eight times in fielding percentage even though he was famous for taking more chances and getting to more grounders than most others.

By 1961 the Orioles were assembling their young stars. The team was beginning to push its way to the top of the American League standings. Although the New York Yankees were still winning pennants, some major changes were taking place among other teams in the league. Cleveland and Chicago, who had challenged the Yankees in the 1950s, were slipping. The new challengers included Minnesota and Baltimore. Baltimore finished third in 1961, a season in which Brooks batted .287 and won another fielding championship. In 1962 the Orioles faltered, but Brooks had his first .300 season (he hit .303) and the Orioles added first baseman Boog Powell to the starting line-up. In 1963 Luis Aparicio joined the team as the shortstop, and the Orioles' infielders won three of the league's four fielding championships.

Then came 1964, and the Yankees won their last pennant. The Orioles finished a close third. Brooks hit .317 and led the league in runs-batted-in with 118. He also led the league's third basemen in put-outs, assists, double plays and fielding average. He was voted the American League's Most Valuable Player.

"We knew we were on the way, once 1964 was finished," Brooks said. "But we needed one more power hitter. We had added such players as Paul Blair and Curt Blefary, and such pitchers as Jim Palmer and Dave McNally. We thought 1965 was going to bring our first pennant."

But the Minnesota Twins, led by Zoilo Versalles and Tony Oliva, edged out the Orioles and White Sox in a tight, three-way pennant race, and the Orioles had to wait until 1966. Before the season started Baltimore completed a trade with Cincinnati which brought outfielder Frank Robinson to the Orioles. Robinson was the man the Orioles needed. He was an established superstar who had won the 1961 MVP award in the National League and was a consistent and powerful hitter.

What a year it was for the Orioles. Frank Robinson won the American League's Triple Crown by leading all hitters in average (.316), home runs (49) and RBI's (122). He combined with big Boog Powell (.287, 34 homers and 109 RBI's) and Brooks Robinson, who contributed a .269 average, 23 homers and 100 RBI's. Between them, Baltimore's Big Three hit 106 homers and drove in 331 runs.

The Orioles led the league from the start of the season and won the pennant by nine games. Then they humiliated the proud Los Angeles Dodgers by sweeping the World Series in four games, beating such pitchers as Sandy Koufax and Don Drysdale.

In 1967 and 1968 the Orioles floundered, puzzling all the experts by not repeating as league champions. In 1969 they won again, but were upset by the New York Mets in the World Series.

"We knew then that we had a good team that could be a great one," Brooks said. "We had to concentrate more, we had to learn to bear down. Winning the 1969 pennant was too easy. We needed something like that World Series to show us the right way to behave. Togetherness, that's what we needed."

The Orioles learned their lesson and won American League pennants in 1970 and 1971.

There was another side to Brooks Robinson besides his on-the-field heroics. Off the field he was a concerned and helpful person. In 1966, after the four-game World Series sweep, Brooks was part of a baseball group which traveled to Vietnam to visit the American soldiers.

"Those kids over there are just unbelievable," Brooks said when he returned. "I came home feeling a great deal of respect for our boys. I just couldn't believe they could be there, do the job they have to do and keep such a high morale going."

When it was announced that Brooks was going to Vietnam, several Baltimore fans asked him to visit their sons in battle. One such soldier was on a night mission when Brooks arrived at Da Nang. Brooks stayed overnight so that he could greet the soldier when he returned the next morning. When Brooks returned to Baltimore, he called the families of the men he had visited.

Robinson was also active in community affairs around Baltimore. He was chairman of the Baltimore County Cancer Crusade and director of the Maryland Chamber of the National Multiple Sclerosis Society. In baseball he was the Orioles' player representative in dealings with team owners and the league.

After his fantastic performance in the 1970 World Series, Brooks came back in 1971 to lead the Orioles to another pennant. He batted .272, drove in 92 runs and finished a few percentage points behind the league's leading third baseman in fielding average. Once again the Orioles finished far ahead of their division. Then they defeated the West Division champ, Oakland, in the playoffs and entered the World Series against Pittsburgh as heavy favorites. But the Series was more like 1969 than 1970. Baltimore won the first two games, but then the Pirates won four of the next five to take the world championship. Brooks batted .318 and

Even Brooks Robinson isn't perfect. Here he bobbles Bob Robertson's grounder during the 1971 World Series.

drove in five runs, but it was not enough.

Manager Weaver had just one worry about Brooks Robinson. He wouldn't take a rest. Most players at his age sat out a few games every month, but Brooks refused.

"If I don't give him a rest once in a while, he'll wear down," Weaver said. "He gets tired and I think that accounts for the slumps he gets into. But he fights and argues. He says he's getting paid to play, not to rest. He says he can rest all winter. I remember once when I forced him to sit out the second game of a doubleheader. He was so miserable on the bench he drove the other guys crazy. He'd sing songs and pace back and forth and yell at the players on the field. He's too tense to rest. I guess it's better if he plays. At least we get some peace and quiet in the dugout."

Brooks had established major league records for most years leading in games played by a third baseman; most years leading the league in fielding average; most lifetime double plays by a third baseman. He held American League marks for third base assists, most games in a season and a career, most career chances and most home runs by a third baseman. He played in eleven All-Star games.

Every year he played he promised to set new records, rewriting the books for third basemen. And at the age of 35 he had shown no intention of quitting soon. Although he was becoming a wealthy man, with interests in sporting goods, banking and other businesses, he still felt that his first business was leading the Orioles in quest of more pennants.

"We have a great team," manager Earl Weaver once said, "because we have great players. And I think that Brooks at third base makes the team come to-

Robinson (right) and Boog Powell congratulate each other after a big win.

gether. There are so many things he does well, it's impossible to put them all down on paper. He's just the greatest third baseman in the history of baseball. That's counting everybody."

INDEX

PICTURE CREDITS: Camera 5: 23 (Dick Darcy), 134 (Ken Regan); United Press International: front and back endpapers, vi–vii, 8, 19, 28, 30, 36–37, 50, 55, 61, 65, 68–69, 75, 93, 96, 102, 110–111, 113, 126–127; Wide World Photos: ii–iii, viii–ix, 4, 13, 33, 44, 47, 58, 67, 77, 79, 84, 86, 88, 99, 104, 115, 118, 121, 124, 132. Cover: Martin Blumenthal, SPORT Magazine.

ABOUT THE AUTHOR

Dave Klein is a sports reporter and columnist for the Newark *Star-Ledger* and the Newhouse newspapers. He is the author of *The Vince Lombardi Story* and other books. This is his first book for young readers. He lives in Scotch Plains, N.J., with his wife and two children.